# ATHENIAN TRIREME
## VS
# PERSIAN TRIREME

## The Graeco-Persian Wars 499–449 BC

## NIC FIELDS

OSPREY PUBLISHING
Bloomsbury Publishing Plc
Kemp House, Chawley Park, Cumnor Hill, Oxford OX2 9PH, UK
29 Earlsfort Terrace, Dublin 2, Ireland
1385 Broadway, 5th Floor, New York, NY 10018, USA
E-mail: info@ospreypublishing.com
**www.ospreypublishing.com**

OSPREY is a trademark of Osprey Publishing Ltd

First published in Great Britain in 2022

A catalogue record for this book is available from the British Library.

ISBN: PB 9781472848611; eBook 9781472848628; ePDF 9781472848635;
XML 9781472848604

22  23  24  25  26   10  9  8  7  6  5  4  3  2  1

Colour artwork illustrations by Adam Hook
Maps by Bounford.com
Index by Angela Hall
Typeset by PDQ Digital Media Solutions, Bungay, UK
Printed and bound in India by Replika Press Private Ltd.

### Artist's note

Readers may care to note that the original paintings from which the colour
plates in this book were prepared are available for private sale. All reproduction
copyright whatsoever is retained by the publishers. All enquiries should be
addressed to:

Scorpio, 158 Mill Road, Hailsham, East Sussex BN27 2SH, UK
Email: scorpiopaintings@btinternet.com

The publishers regret that they can enter into no correspondence upon
this matter.

Front cover (above): An Athenian trireme under sail. (Adam Hook)
Front cover (below): A Phoenician trireme in Persian service. (Adam Hook)

Title page photograph: Fragment of a gypsum bas-relief (London, British
Museum) from South-West Palace, Room VII, panel 11, Nineveh, and dated
*c.*701 BC. The starboard side of a Phoenician warship with a pointed forefoot
sheathed (in metal) as a waterline ram and pulled at two levels. There are eight
oarsmen whose heads and shoulders are visible between stanchions in an open
level. Below this level eight oars, *en échelon*, emerge through oar ports.
However, above the open level and below the deck bulwark hung with shields
there is a further level represented by alternate open and latticework spaces.
Though shown unmanned, this upper level could accommodate a third file of
oarsman and so it does seem valid to argue that the warship represents an early,
if not the first, design of a trireme. (World Imaging/Wikimedia Commons/
CC BY-SA 3.0)

Osprey Publishing supports the Woodland Trust, the UK's leading woodland
conservation charity.

To find out more about our authors and books visit
**www.ospreypublishing.com**. Here you will find extracts, author interviews,
details of forthcoming events and the option to sign up for our newsletter.

### Editor's note

In most cases imperial measurements, including nautical miles (NM), knots
(kn) and long tons, have been used in this book. For ease of comparison please
refer to the following conversion table:

1 NM = 1.85km
1yd = 0.9m
1ft = 0.3m
1in = 2.54cm/25.4mm
1kn = 1.85km/h
1 long ton = 1.02 metric tonnes
1lb = 0.45kg

# CONTENTS

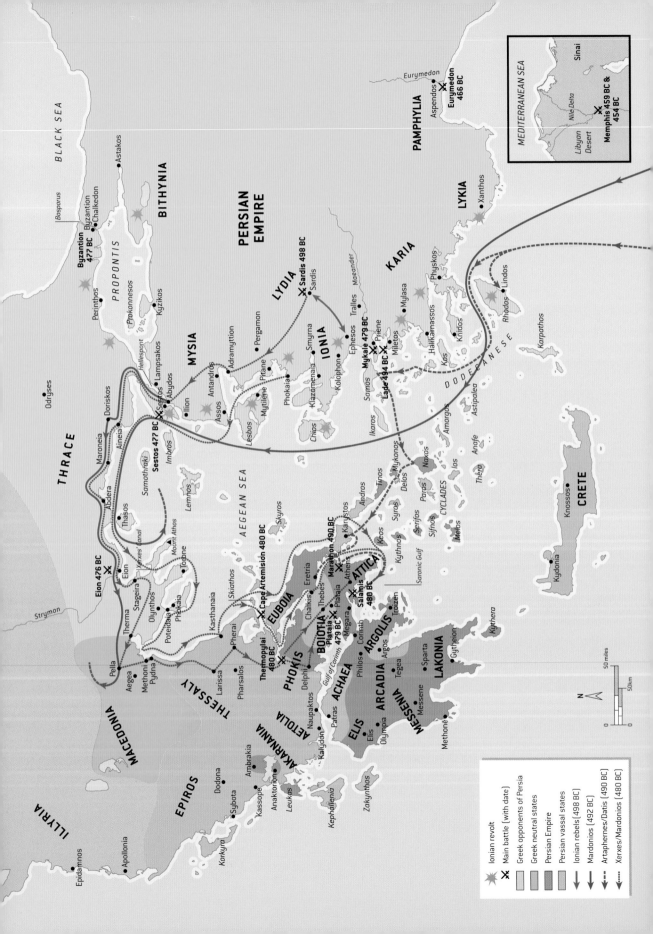

# INTRODUCTION

Unsurprisingly, the oldest written histories are all about war, and the founding texts of western historiography deal with three wars – the Trojan, the Graeco-Persian, and the Peloponnesian. Our story concerns the second of these, the Graeco-Persian wars, or what the Greeks called *Mēdiká*, the 'Median war' (e.g. Thuc. 1.23.1). This story is told in fine style by Herodotos, the 'father of history'.

The rise of Persia was swift and spectacular. Within a generation it absorbed Media, crushed Lydia, and, after the surrender of Babylon, was able to win Egypt with very little fighting. As for the Greeks, they first came into conflict with the 'arrow-bearing Medes' in Aegean Anatolia, as a result of the conquest of Lydia by Kyros II, otherwise known as 'the Great' (r. 559–530 BC), probably in 546 BC. Though Lydia had been the up-and-coming kingdom in Anatolia, there were Greek *poleis* ('city-states') on this side of the Aegean Sea and, following an abortive Lydian revolt in which some of the Anatolian Greeks participated, many of their *poleis* were taken by assault, and the rest were ordered to bend the knee to Achaemenid Persian rule, or else.

In the early years of the 5th century BC there was a widespread rebellion from Byzantion to Karia, in which Cyprus joined, what we call the Ionian Revolt (499–494 BC). Initially the Anatolian Greeks were surprisingly successful. This appears in part to have been due to the sluggishness of Persian mobilization. The rebels solicited aid in mainland Greece, but only Athens with 20 warships filled with hoplites and Eretria with five responded and they soon departed without engaging the Persian fleet in battle; presumably at this time, as Thucydides (1.14.3) emphasizes, the Athenian navy consisted mainly of *pentēkóntoroi*, the standard 50-oared ship of the period, and a few triremes (Gk. *trlērēs/ triērēis*, Lat. *triremis/ triemise*), if any. In the hinterland of Anatolia, with the advantage of interior lines of communication and superior numbers, the Persians were able to operate in more than one theatre of operations at once, and to use the river valleys as a means of attack, whereas communications were more difficult for the Anatolian Greeks.

Five land battles are recorded by Herodotos, in four of which the Persians were victorious, but almost no details have survived (no account has survived in the Persian records), save at Malēne where the Persian cavalry somehow played the decisive role. The one battle the Greeks managed to win was when they ambushed a Persian force at night. Meanwhile, despite a Greek victory at sea off the island, Cyprus was re-conquered. The decisive Persian victory was also at sea, off Lade, which was followed by the capture of nearby Miletos, the nerve centre of the revolt, probably in 494 BC. The Persians went on to conquer Thrace, including its Greek coastal *poleis*, and even the kingdom of Macedonia.

When the Athenians and Eretrians attacked Sardis, the former capital of the Lydian kingdom, the Persians caught the Athenians and Eretrians as they made for their ships and beat them in battle; the Athenian *dēmos* ('people') voted to have no more to do with the Ionian Revolt. Even so, the burning of Sardis did result, in 490 BC, in the first Persian attack on Greece proper. A fleet of perhaps 600 ships, carrying possibly some 25,000 troops, including cavalry, first subdued the Cyclades, and then took Karystos and Eretria on Euboia. But when the expeditionary force landed at Marathon, the Athenians, with Plataian support, drove the Persians back to their ships.

Ten years later, in 480 BC, the Persians were back, this time overland by way of Thrace and Macedonia, and led by the Great King, Xerxes, in person. Herodotos

The extreme sharpness of a Greek oared ship can be appreciated from this 5th-century BC bronze votive lamp (Athens, National Archaeological Museum, inv. 7038) in the shape of a trireme from the Erechteion on the Acropolis of Athens. It bears the inscription Ἱερὸν τῆς Ἀθηνᾶς, 'sanctuary of Athena'; the lamp was most probably a votive offering from a *triērarchos*. With its straight strong keel, low freeboard, shapely upswept stern, and projecting bronze-sheathed ram, the Athenian trireme looked every inch a graceful ship-killer. Triremes were a huge technical advance, allowing Athens to build its maritime empire and dominate the Aegean in the 5th century BC. (Tilemachos Efthimiadis/Wikimedia Commons/ CC BY-SA 3.0)

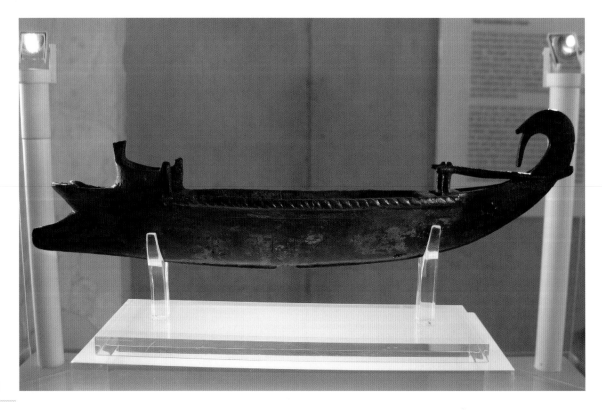

# XERXES, GREAT KING OF PERSIA (r. 486–465 BC)

At the beginning of his reign, Xerxes crushed a revolt in Egypt (485 BC) and later there was similar trouble in Babylonia (the precise year is uncertain, but 481 BC is probable). Plans for an expedition against Greece were inherited from Dareios. Having reached natural boundaries to north, east, and south, the only direction for the empire to expand was to the west. Although he fought successfully in central Asia, Xerxes is celebrated for his failure to conquer Greece and the loss of Macedonia, Thrace, and Aegean Anatolia and the double defeat at the Eurymedon River.

The expedition against the Greeks (to avenge Marathon but also reflecting an expansionist imperative) was elaborately prepared (the Hellespont bridged, a canal cut through the peninsula of Mount Athos, rivers were bridged, roads were improved, and food dumps established at selective points on the invasion route, as they were in Thrace and Macedonia), and large scale. Herodotos' picture of a colossal army incorporating every ethnically diverse part of the Achaemenid empire is quantitatively nonsensical, but there are no non-Greek sources specific to the period and views diverge on how to replace it. Even if it did not suffer from gigantisms, there is little doubt that Xerxes' invasion force was extraordinarily large (and unwieldy) and its logistical demands required a strategy of co-ordinated land-sea advance along the coast that was ill suited to Greek topography. There is also a suspicion that too much reliance was placed on expected Greek disunity. The campaign foundered at Salamis, where Xerxes confidently anticipated the Greeks' destruction, his fleet fought on Greek terms, while Plataia again illustrated the advantage Greek hoplites had over the lighter armed Persian infantry when numerical superiority and cavalry mobility were neutralized by terrain.

Xerxes' reputation as a weakling and a womaniser depends on certain recognisably novelistic passages in Herodotos (7.2–3, 9.108–13) and on the reading of royal inscriptions as personal messages by the Great Kings, rather than as formulaic royal statements. The Greeks may have cast Xerxes as the barbarian at the gate, but it should be noted that seen from the heartland of his empire, his reign forms a period of consolidation, not of incipient decay. For despite Xerxes' land and naval forces seeking to bring the Greeks to heel only to fail time and again on land and sea, the empire proved significantly robust to survive and prosper.

Xerxes, together with his eldest son Dareios, was murdered during a palace *coup d'état* in 465 BC. This was led by Artabanos, a Hyrkanian by birth and the commander of the royal bodyguard, after the eunuch Mithridates, the royal chamberlain, gave him access to the king's bedchamber (Arist. *Pol*. 5.1311b37–40, Diod. 11.69.1–2).

Detail of the relief of Xerxes, façade of the Tomb of Xerxes, Naqš-e Rustam, Iran. It depicts a life-size Xerxes, robed and armed with his composite recurve bow. (A. Davey/Wikimedia Commons/CC BY-SA 2.0)

estimates 1.7 million fighting men crossed the Hellespont, 7.60.1), but modern scholarship estimates it numbered 60,000–70,000 men including about 10,000 horsemen (Lazenby 1993: 92), while Xerxes' navy perhaps contained over a thousand warships.

Resistance in Greece centred on Sparta and its Peloponnesian allies, but Athens also joined the alliance, what modern commentators call the Hellenic League (in truth, a jittery, barely united coalition), with a scattering of other states in central Greece and nearby islands. The Greeks decided to hold Thermopylai, while stationing a fleet at Artemision, some 64km to the east, on the north coast of Euboia. Here for three days the Greeks more than held their own, although the losses they sustained and the fall of Thermopylai eventually compelled withdrawal.

Most of central Greece now more or less willingly went over to Xerxes, but the citizens of the Boiotian *poleis* of Thespiai and Plataia sought refuge in the Peloponnese, and now if not before, the citizens of Athens, too, were evacuated. The Hellenic League fleet took station off Salamis, and it was here that the first decisive encounter of the war took place. The Persian fleet ventured into the narrow channel between the island and the mainland, perhaps as a result of a message from the Athenian *stratēgós*, Themistokles, and was badly mauled. It still possibly had more ships than the Greeks, but its morale had gone, and it now withdrew to Anatolia, followed by Xerxes himself. But the Persian army still remained undefeated, and Xerxes probably left the bulk of his land forces behind, under his very able cousin and brother-in-law, Mardonios.

Having wintered in Thessaly, Mardonios marched south again in the late spring, compelling the re-evacuation of Attica. Despite some procrastination, the Spartans realized their defences across the Isthmus would not save them if the Athenian navy passed under Persian control, and mobilized their army. Mardonios fell back to Boiotia, and it was here, just outside Plataia, that the final encounter took place, probably in August, when the largest army of hoplites ever assembled, under the Spartan regent Pausanias, annihilated most of Mardonios' Asiatic troops.

For 30 years hostilities continued between Greeks and Persians, and though there were defeats, partial victories, more defeats, and an eventual détente between the two, the Athenian navy was the decisive factor in the successes that were gained.

Stone anchors (Peiraieus, Hellenic Maritime Museum). A common form of anchor was the apsidal stone with a single hole bored through it, a type found from the Bronze Age through to modern times. (José M. Ciordia/Wikimedia Commons/CC BY-SA 4.0)

# CHRONOLOGY

| | |
|---|---|
| **499–494 BC** | Ionian Revolt. |
| **499 BC** | Persians attack Cycladic island of Naxos. |
| **498 BC** | Sardis burnt by Athenians, Eretrians and Milesians. |
| **497 BC** | Persians crush revolt on Cyprus. |
| **494 BC** | Naval battle of Lade. Sack of Miletos by Persians – end of Ionian Revolt. |
| **493/492 BC** | Themistokles elected *árchōn* at Athens. Phrynichos prosecuted in Athens for play *Fall of Miletos*. |
| **493 BC** | Persian victory at Malēne. |
| **492 BC** | Miltiades flees Thracian Chersonese and returns to Athens – prosecuted for tyranny. Mardonios' operations in Thrace end in failure – Dareios I dismisses Mardonios. |
| **491 BC** | Dareios demands all Greek states to submit to his rule. |
| **490 BC** | Persians sack Eretria (Euboia) and deport its citizens. Battle of Marathon. |
| **489 BC** | Miltiades dies of his wounds received on Paros. |
| **486 BC** | Xerxes becomes Great King of Persia. First ostracism in Athens. |
| **485 BC** | Revolt of Egypt. |
| *c.***484 BC** | Birth of Herodotos in Halikarnassos (Karia). |
| **483 BC** | Persians start to dig canal across neck of Mount Athos peninsula. |
| **483/482 BC** | Rich find of silver at Laureion (Attica) with which Themistokles persuades Athenians to build a fleet. |
| *c.***481 BC** | Revolt of Babylonia. |
| **480 BC** | Xerxes invasion of Greece – battles of Artemision, Thermopylai and Salamis. |
| **479 BC** | Battles of Plataia (Boiotia) – Mardonios killed – and Mykale (Ionia) – end of Xerxes' invasion. |
| **478/477 BC** | Foundation of Delian League (modern name), Aegean under Athenian influence. Persians driven from Sestos and Byzantion (Thracian Chersonese). |
| **476 BC** | Persians driven from Eïon (Thrace). |
| **472 BC** | Aischylos wins first prize in Great Dionysia for *Pérsai*. |
| *c.***466 BC** | Athenians under Kimon defeat Persians at the river Eurymedon (Pamphylia). |
| **465 BC** | Assassination of Xerxes. |
| **461 BC** | Ostracism of Kimon. |
| *c.***460 BC** | Thucydides born. |
| **459 BC** | Athenian armada sent to Nile Delta to support Egyptian rebellion. |
| **457 BC** | Battle of Tanagra (Boiotia). |
| **456 BC** | Death of Aischylos in Gela (Sicily). |
| **454 BC** | Athenian fleet destroyed by Persians in Nile Delta. |
| **454/453 BC** | Delian League treasury moved from Delos to Athens. |
| **451 BC** | Athenian expedition to Cyprus – death of Kimon. |
| **449 BC** | Peace of Kallias – *détente* between Athens and Persia. |
| **447/446 BC** | Building of the Parthenon begun. |

# DESIGN AND DEVELOPMENT

## THE FIRST TRIREME

Who built the first triremes, and when, remain contentious questions. Hipponax of Ephesos and later Klazomenai, a 6th-century BC iambic satirist, is the first Greek writer we know of to mention the *triērēs*, trireme. He lampoons a local painter, and scolds him thus:

> Shoulder-deep-slackjaw Mimnes, another time don't paint a snake along a trireme's hull
> that's running back from the prow to tillerman. They'll be ruinous, you berk, you nerd,
> and a bad omen for the tillerman if a snake comes and bites him on the shin. (Hipponax
> fr. 28 West)

Let me translate: the painted snake while intended to serve as an apotropaic sign to frighten the enemy, functions ironically as a bad omen and a potential hazard to the helmsman. In other words, the 'berk' Mimnes had painted his snake back to front.

Hipponax, it should be noted, was writing soon after Ephesos and the rest of the Greek *poleis* in Anatolia had been conquered by the Achaemenid Persians and forced to contribute naval forces to subsequent Persian campaigns of conquest. At this time the major Greek sea powers were using *pentēkóntoroi*, yet at the naval engagement of Lade in 494 BC, six Ionian *poleis* and three eastern Aegean island *poleis* between them could muster 353 fully equipped triremes. This leap in ship building may have been promoted and paid for by the Persians, no seafarers themselves but keen to create a modern imperial navy. Herodotos (5.30.4, 6.8.1) indeed implies as much when he reports that Miletos six years before could not aid the Naxian exiles for lack of ships, while they contributed no less than 80 triremes at Lade.

Meanwhile, on the other side of the Aegean, triremes were a luxury item. Miltiades, whose family was among the most powerful in Athens and had a record of multiple four-horse chariot victories in the pan-Hellenic games at Olympia, sailed 'in a trireme to the (Thracian) Chersonese to take control of the country' (Hdt. 6.39.1) in the capacity of a semi-autonomous tyrant. In 513 BC, Dareios I, the Great King, led an army into Thracian Chersonese (now the Gallipoli peninsula) and forced the region into submission, thereby reducing Miltiades to the rank of an Achaemenid vassal. Having backed the wrong horse during the Ionian Revolt and following its eventual collapse, Miltiades 'sailed back to Athens with five triremes loaded with the possessions that he had nearby' (Hdt. 6.41.1). So, it looks as if the petty autocrat had acquired at least four more triremes while serving the greater interests of Persia. Still, for Miltiades, a risk-taker and adventurer, it was a case of 'he runs on Scylla, wishing to avoid Charybis', for the Athens he returned to with his treasures was no longer a tyranny, but had morphed into a democracy.

For the naval effort against Xerxes' invasion Kleinias, son of Alkibiades, 'brought to the war 200 men and a ship of his own, all at his own expense' (Hdt. 8.17). However, Kleinias, like Miltiades before him, hailed from one of the richest families in Athens and Herodotos mentions the occurrence because it was exceptional. Kleinias may have been the last Athenian to contribute a private ship to the Athenian fleet, even the last Athenian to own a warship at all. The difficulty and cost of fitting and maintaining a trireme rather than a *pentēkóntoros*, and recruiting and provisioning a crew of 200, rather than 50, put the trireme beyond the reach of all but the very richest of private citizens. Trireme navies and all that they necessitated were to be a matter of civic expense.

Thucydides (1.13.2–3, cf. Plin. *HN* 7.57), who himself commanded triremes in the Peloponnesian War (431–404 BC), credits the Corinthians as being the *first of the Greeks* to build triremes, and 300 years before the end of the war (either the Peace of Nikias, or the end of the Peloponnesian War, viz. 721 BC or 704 BC) Ameinokles, a Corinthian shipwright, built four triremes for the Samians, though it must be emphasized the Samians were still using a greater number of *pentēkóntoroi* than triremes as late as 540 BC (Hdt. 3.39.2, 3.44.2). Even so, there is a gap of a good 150 years between Ameinokles' triremes and Hipponax's poetic reference to a trireme. The Corinthians' role in developing the trireme was widely believed in the Greek world. Diodorus Siculus (14.41.3, cf. 14.42.2, 14.44.7), writing in the 1st century BC but using earlier sources, informs us Dionysios I of Syracuse associated the Corinthians with the *first* triremes, and was therefore eager to build the *first* quadriremes (Gk. *tetrēreis*) and quinqueremes

Detail on the Apulian red-figure volute krater (Napoli, Museo Archeologico Nazionale, inv. 81947) from Canosa, known as the Darius Vase and dated to 340–320 BC. Dareios I (r. 521–486 BC) is enthroned while holding audience in his court (note ΔΑΡΕΙΟΣ, top right). Dareios (OP *Dārayavauš*), the last Great King to significantly add to the Achaemenid empire, was a self-made man who took power in a *coup d'etat*: a wise and magnificent monarch, he went on to become a great conqueror, a brilliant administrator, and an architectural genius. The Athenians, however, liked to tell how Dareios had called for his war bow when he learned that they had helped to burn Sardis. Having fitted an arrow to the string, the king shot it high into the sky, a ritual action to seal an oath of vengeance. Turning to his cupbearer, he commanded him to whisper thrice in his ear whenever he sat down for dinner the words, 'Master, remember the Athenians' (Hdt. 5.105). (Carlo Raso/Wikimedia Commons/CC BY-SA 2.0)

11

Scaled wooden model of a Phoenician warship (Haifa, Israeli National Maritime Museum) based on those depicted in the South-West Palace bas-relief. (Bukvoed/Wikimedia Commons/ CC BY-SA 4.0)

Ma'agan Mikha'el ship (Haifa, University of Haifa Hecht Museum), a well-preserved 5th-century BC merchantman discovered off the coast of Kibbutz Ma'agan Mikha'el, some 30km south of Haifa, in September 1985. The well preserved hull, built shell-first using pegged mortise-and-tenon joints, is 11.25m long and 4m wide, with an estimated displacement weight of 25 tons, over 12 of which was ballast. The keel consists of a single timber 8.5m long, 11cm wide and 16cm high. The hull planking (4cm thick), stem and sternpost, longitudinal springers, frames, vertical stanchions, keel, and mast step, were all constructed using Aleppo pine, except for the tenons and the false keel attached to the keel. (Oren Rozen/Wikimedia Commons/ CC BY-SA 3.0)

(Gk. *pentēreis*) in Syracuse, a former colony of Corinth and currently a centre of innovative technology. Corinth itself not only had a long tradition of naval pioneering, but its former colony and now maritime rival Korkyra had been building triremes before the Athenians had started (Thuc. 1.14.2), and in 480 BC possessed at least 60 triremes (Hdt. 7.168.2). Nevertheless, the Greek view does not militate against the opinion that triremes were invented by the Phoenicians in the 8th century BC.

According to Herodotos (1.143.1), when the Persians came into contact with the Greeks after they had annexed Lydia around 546 BC, they did not have a navy. In truth, the Persians only possessed an instrument for their maritime policy when they had established their authority over the maritime cities of Phoenicia. Herodotos notes the Phoenicians took service under Kambyses 'of their own free will, and his whole naval power was dependent on them' (3.19.3). In brief, never a seapower itself, Achaemenid Persia put its confidence in the Phoenicians, which is one of the fundamental points we need to recognize.

Clemens Alexandrinus, a late 2nd-century AD Christian theologian, makes the claim (*Strom.* 1.16.76.7) that the invention of the trireme (*tríkroton*, 'three-banked ship') should be attributed to the Sidonians. Clemens sounds very authoritative here, but what he provides us with is nothing more than a quick list of 53 inventions attributed to 'barbarians'. As you would have thought, there are modern commentators who argue this is a muddled diatribe which is highly questionable at best (e.g. Lloyd 1975: 49–50). Still, the answer to the question of where the trireme was first invented may lie not in our written primary sources but in one set of Assyrian bas-reliefs from the turn of the 7th century BC, more of which presently.

The Phoenicians collectively were of course the foremost mariners of antiquity and recorded as such in the Old Testament (1 Kgs. 9:27, Ezek. 27:4). The Phoenicians were the first mariners to circumnavigate Africa, as recorded by Herodotos (4.42.3–4), in a journey that took three years by sailing west round the Cape of Good Hope. In August 2008, *Phoenicia*, a reconstructed 20m-long Phoenician trading vessel built on Arwad Island using traditional methods and construction techniques, was launched, and the recreation of the circumnavigation of Africa was completed in October 2010. A voyage of over 32,187km, this was arguably the longest voyage in a reconstruction of an ancient ship in distance and time.

We may surmise with some confidence that when it came to ships the Phoenicians naturally followed their own shipbuilding traditions. What we gather from pictorial reliefs is that the Phoenician trireme was roughly the same length as its Athenian counterpart but it was wider and probably higher too. Athenian triremes were not fully decked until comparatively late. A continuous deck extending right across the ship cannot, for reasons of stability, be reconciled with a long narrow ship such as the Athenian trireme. In order to carry extra marines, Phoenician triremes needed continuous decks, which were lined with bulwarks to protect the fighting complement. The outside of the deck was hung along the edge with a row of shields. The bronze-sheathed waterline ram was long, conical and tapering instead of stubby and

# THE PHOENICIANS

A recent academic work has taken aim at the entire edifice of Phoenician history and culture. In doing so the author has made a decisive case which supports the premise that the Phoenicians did not exist as a self-conscious collective or coherent ethno-cultural group above the socio-political level of their own city-state. The 'Phoenician people, or civilization, or nation, is not actually a real historical object, but rather a product of the scholarly and political ideologies … thoroughly interwoven with ideas about the modern nation-state' (Quinn 2018: 24). This is predominantly so with regards to postcolonial Lebanon, where the newly liberated Lebanese looked to the Phoenicians as ancestral people from which they came, not least in order to assert that their identity was wholly distinct from that of the Arabs, a self-consciousness that lingered on until the catastrophe of the civil war that erupted in 1975. It is certainly true that no one ever called her- or himself 'Phoenician' in Phoenician, for the ethnic name *phoinix* is a Greek invention, which not only denoted a date palm but the mysterious bird called the phoenix, as well as a deep red dye.

There are serious grounds for hesitation, for it certainly looks as if the 'Phoenician-speakers defined themselves, at least in their inscriptions, in terms of their cities and, even more, their families' (Quinn 2018: 26). In the Old Testament there is no reference to the Greek term φοῖνιξ: instead, the inhabitants of the Levantine coastal cities are identified by their city of origin, most often as *tsīydōnīy*, Sidonians (e.g. Gen. 10:15, Judg. 3:3, 10:12, 18:7, 1 Kgs. 5:6, 11:1, 16:31). The Achaemenid Persians, who controlled the region from 539 BC to 332 BC, certainly treated these cities as relatively autonomous political entities within the satrapy known as *Ebir-nāri*, 'beyond the river (Euphrates)', which also included Palestine and Cyprus. While this may be so, for the sole purpose of convenience, the blanket term 'Phoenician' will be used throughout as a label to designate those mariners who hailed from Arados, Byblos, Sidon, and Tyre, the four Levantine coastal cities that fielded substantial naval fleets for Achaemenid Persia.

There is no doubt that the Phoenicians were prominent in the ancient Mediterranean. They were famous for seafaring and commerce. As we are reminded by Homer, the generic Phoenicians were 'famous seafarers' (*Od.* 15.415), and Herodotos' Phoenicians are people of the sea from their first appearance in the first chapter of book one.

Ma'agan Mikha'el ship anchor (Haifa, University of Haifa Hecht Museum). The ship's one-armed anchor made from lead-filled oak was discovered off the vessel's starboard side, with the remains of rope still attached to the crown and lifting loop. The anchor's body was carved from a single timber, as was the stock. The wood used in its construction was identical to the oak used on the ship's tenons. A tooth made of copper had almost corroded away. The Ma'agan Mikha'el anchor is the first complete one-armed ancient wooden anchor ever discovered. (Hanay/Wikimedia Commons/ CC BY-SA 3.0)

three-pronged. In addition to the clear differences between those of Athens and those of Phoenicia, there are some scholars who believe the trireme was of Phoenician origin and not of Greek.

Around the time of the Neo-Assyrian king Sennacherib (r. 705–681 BC), a vigorous campaigner and enthusiastic palace builder, the Phoenicians introduced the practice of placing oarsmen on two different levels, one above the other, and thus for a vessel of the same length, doubling the number of oarsmen. Vessels of this type, which the Greeks described as *díkrotos* (Eur. *IT* 408, cf. Xen. *Hell.* 2.1.28) and there is a hint of the two-level system in the *Iliad* (2.509–10),[1] are visibly seen on a gypsum bas-relief from the Southwest Palace at Nineveh (Kuyundjik, opposite Mosul). Here, the inhabitants of a Phoenician city appear to be fleeing at the moment their city is about to fall and so escape their enemy: in 701 BC Sennacherib attacked the Phoenician maritime cities of Tyre and Sidon. The sculptor of this incredibly detailed piece of Assyrian artwork, which illustrates the evacuations of Tyre and Sidon by King Lulī, credits the Phoenicians with a type of oared warship remarkably similar to a trireme.

In actuality, the 11 ships shown in the bas-relief are of two distinct types. All 11 ships have four characteristics in common: they all have a row of shields in the Tyrian manner (Ezek. 27:10); they are all fully decked; they all have a double level of oars, which are staggered, an upper oar centred over the space between two of the lower ones; and all are guided by two steering oars thrust out from the stern.

On the other hand, whereas six ships are each without mast or rigging, and are each rounded off in the same way both at stem and stern, the other five each have a mast, positioned about midship, a yard hung across it, and a sail with loose brailings close reefed to this yard. They have large circular shields (eight to ten) fastened around their superstructures. Their bows are each equipped with a long projecting beak, like an old-fashioned wooden ploughshare, just below the waterline. The vertical lines near the aft end of one of these projections imply metal sheathing, which would suggest this is a ram and not a cutwater (Basch 1969: 147), though some recent scholarship has challenged this view (Mark 2008: 257). Some marines armed with spears stand on the decks. The oarsmen, in both types of vessel, are represented as only eight or ten per side, but this probably arose from artistic licence.

Clearly the first type of vessel is a Phoenician merchantman, the second a Phoenician warship. While the bas-relief may only represent the later as a bireme, there is a top level where a third level of oars could be utilized. If this is the case, and the trireme was invented in Sidon, it does imply that Clemens Alexandrinus was

---

1 The Greek term *diērēs* (Lat. *biremis*, bireme) does not appear until the 2nd century AD in the grammarian Pollux.

# PHOENICIAN TRIREME

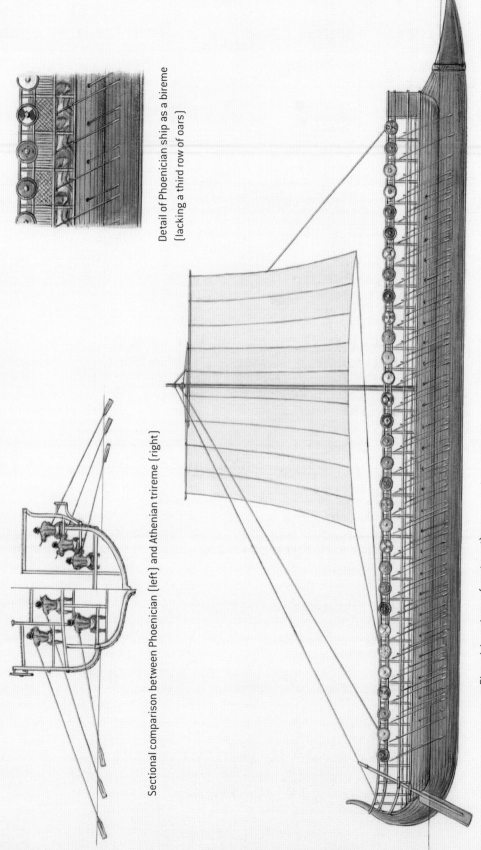

Detail of Phoenician ship as a bireme (lacking a third row of oars)

Sectional comparison between Phoenician (left) and Athenian trireme (right)

Phoenician trireme (starboard)

The Phoenician trireme is problematic: there is a question as to whether or not it is indeed a bireme (two banks of oars) or a trireme (three banks of oars). The answer is both, that is to say, it appears the Phoenician trireme was first a bireme-cum-proto-trireme. Phoenician vessels are shown here with both three and two banks of oars.

Full-scale reconstruction of the Ma'agan Mikha'el ship, built by Ya'acov Kahanov and a team from the University of Haifa. She was launched on 28 December 2016. Initially believed to have been a Phoenician vessel, in view of its construction and contents, the original ship is now deemed to be Cypriot in origin. (Wikimedia Commons/ CC BY-SA 3.0)

correct. However, it was the Athenians, with their newly found wealth from the Attic silver mines, who constructed a trireme navy large enough to hold sway over the Aegean.

# SILVER AND SHIPS

To Athens in the 5th century BC the importance of the *triērēs* hardly needs to be emphasized. The fleet of 200 *triereis* built shortly before Xerxes' invasion appeared on the horizon (when it was involved in a naval war with its island neighbour Aegina, a prosperous naval and commercial power situated in the Saronic Gulf) enabled the Hellenic League successfully to repel the invasion when it came. The entrance fee to the club of naval powers was high, and we are told that Athens was only able to afford it by using, at Themistokles' suggestion, the proceeds of a lucky strike in the silver mines of Laureion. These ships were also, Plutarch tells us, specially designed by Themistokles 'for speed and quick turning' (*Kim.* 12.2), information which suggests that he had his own ideas of *triērēs* tactics, though Thucydides, a near contemporary of Themistokles, says 'even these ships still did not have complete decks' (1.14.3), that is, there was a sizeable gap running down the middle of the trireme. So, what we are looking at here is a light wooden canopy, whose main purpose would have been to stop javelins and arrows plunging into the oarsmen as well as to carry a small number of marines, who would

# THEMISTOKLES (c.524–459 BC)

By 483 BC Themistokles was the most influential politician in Athens, and as he believed that the Persians would return, he favoured the expansion of the Athenian navy to meet the next threat. Aristeides (widely known as 'the Just'), his most bitter of political opponents, strongly opposed this course of action. Themistokles' naval policy prevailed – he persuaded the Athenians to allocate the one hundred talents generated by the new silver mines at Laureion (483/482 BC) on building new ships and, thus, the navy grew from seventy to 200 triremes, and Aristeides was ostracized (Hdt. 7.144.1–2, Arist. [*Ath. pol.*] 22.7).

When the Persians returned to Greece, they handily trounced King Leonidas at Thermopylai and occupied Athens. Themistokles had evacuated the Athenians to Troizen on the opposite side of the Saronic Gulf to Athens and to the nearby island of Salamis (Hdt. 8.41.1, Plut. *Them*. 10.3). It was off the latter location where he engaged and destroyed the Persian fleet – although the Greek fleet had been entrusted to the Spartan naval commander Eurybiades, it was Themistokles who had determined the strategy of the day. Besides, Spartan admiral or not, the Athenian triremes made up the bulk of the Hellenic League fleet. Whether or not he did spread misinformation that the Greeks were already more than half beaten on the eve of Salamis, thereby manipulating the Persian fleet – both Herodotos and Aischylos allege he did so – Themistokles became a national hero.

Themistokles enjoyed a post-war period of respect from his fellow citizens. But he soon began to lose the confidence of the *dēmos*, his power and prestige creating jealous enemies, and his own arrogance and his alleged readiness to take bribes would be his undoing. Diodorus Siculus and Plutarch both refer to some accusation levelled against him and sometime between 476 BC and 471 BC he was ostracized (Diod. Sic. 11.55.1, Plut. *Them*. 22.3), a relatively honourable device by which a prominent man was removed from Athens for ten years. Worse was to come, however, for Themistokles suffered an additional strike, namely *atīmíā*, outlawry. This latter penalty meant in effect condemnation as a public enemy, which entailed confiscation of a man's property and even exposed his immediate family to the dangers of prosecution.

When the Spartans further accused him of treasonable intrigues with Persia (Diod. Sic. 11.55.4), he fled to Korkyra, thence to Admeitos of Molossia, and finally to the Persian empire. He was proclaimed a traitor at Athens and his property was confiscated. Themistokles was well received in the court of Artaxerxes I (r. 465–425 BC), and was graciously allowed to settle in Magnesia on the Maeander, where he served as the Persian governor (Akk. *ša rēš šarri*, 'master'). Themistokles died at Magnesia aged 65.

Marble portrait bust of Themistokles (Ostia Antica, Museo Ostiense), a Roman copy of a 5th-century BC Greek original. (Sailko/Wikimedia Commons/CC BY-SA 3.0)

Silver coin of Themistokles (Bibliothèque nationale de France) as the Persian governor of Magnesia on the Maeander, dated c.465–459 BC. On the obverse is Apollo standing in a *chlamýs* and holding a sceptre with a barley stalk. The legend around reads ΘΕΜΙΣΤΟΚ-ΛΕΟΣ (Themistokles). On the reverse is a flying raven (an attribute of Apollo) with the letters M–A (Magnesia) beneath. Early writers often unfavourably view Themistokles. Admittedly a master strategist, he is often depicted as a slick politician with an itching palm, bent on enriching himself even during the crisis of Xerxes' invasion. (Gallica Digital Library, BnF/Wikimedia Commons/CCO 1.0)

have been sitting or reclining (more of which later). Only by understanding these tactics and the nature of the ships which employed them can we form an idea of how in 480 BC the Greeks were able to defeat a fleet initially three times the size of their own.

It was back in 483/482 BC, according to Herodotos (7.144.1) and the author of the Ἀθηναίων πολιτεία (22.7), that Athens had the good fortune to strike an unusually rich vein of silver, 100 Attic-Euboic talents worth (Gk. *tálanton*, equivalent to 6,000 Attic drachmae and comparable to 26.2kg), in the Laureion mines of south-east Attica. On the proposal of Themistokles, the Athenian *dēmos*, who owned the mines collectively, voted to use this silver bonanza to construct a fleet 'of 200 warships for use in the war with Aegina' (Hdt. 7.144.1, cf. Arist. [*Ath. pol.*] 22.7 and Plut. *Them.* 4.2, who reckon 100 triremes) instead of distributing it as cash transfers to all citizens. In the previous war with Aegina, its naval rival across the Saronic Gulf, Athens could only call upon 70 triremes, 20 of which had been 'rented' from Corinth at 'five drachmae apiece' (Hdt. 6.89). On the eve of Xerxes' invasion, having performed a labour fit for the monster-slayer hero Herakles (Hercules), the Athenians had at least 200 triremes of their own fully equipped and ready for service (Hdt. 8.1.1, 8.14.1, 8.44.1). It was these Athenian triremes that formed the bulk of the naval arm of Hellenic League, and consequently were to play a major role in the victory at Salamis. In Aischylos' *Pérsai*, a play in support of the hero of Salamis, Themistokles, the lament of the Persian chorus, composed of aged and venerable Persian councillors, can be taken as a capsule summary: 'They have a spring of silver treasured in their soil' (238, cf. 743).

If Plutarch is correct, in his naval bill Themistokles had specified that Athens' new warship should be fast triremes: light and open for greater speed and manoeuvrability. To reiterate, only a simple canopy deck (without guardrails) connected the helmsman's small quarterdeck to the foredeck at the prow where the bow officer was stationed. A gangway ran down the middle of the trireme, giving access to the interior. The new Athenian triremes were designed for ramming attacks, not for carrying large contingents of fighting men. By committing themselves completely to this design, Themistokles and his fellow Athenians were taking a calculated risk. For many naval actions, both at sea and of an amphibious nature, fully decked triremes would have been more serviceable. Time would tell whether Athens had made the right choice.

# ATHENIAN TRIREME

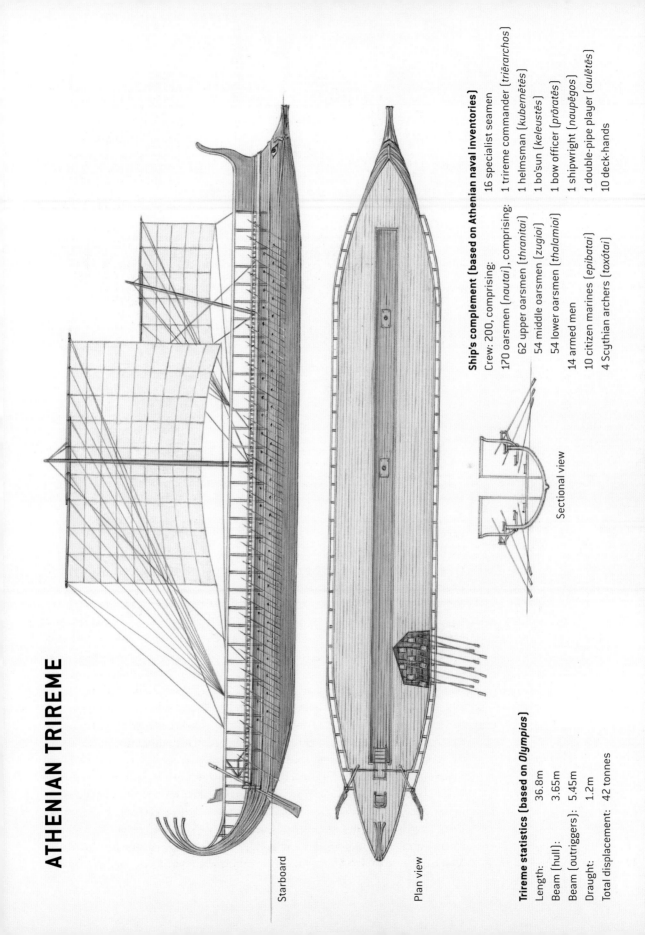

Starboard

Plan view

Sectional view

**Trireme statistics (based on *Olympias*)**

| | |
|---|---|
| Length: | 36.8m |
| Beam (hull): | 3.65m |
| Beam (outriggers): | 5.45m |
| Draught: | 1.2m |
| Total displacement: | 42 tonnes |

**Ship's complement (based on Athenian naval inventories)**

Crew: 200, comprising:

| | |
|---|---|
| 170 oarsmen (*nautai*), comprising: | 16 specialist seamen |
| 62 upper oarsmen (*thranitai*) | 1 trireme commander (*triērarchos*) |
| 54 middle oarsmen (*zugioi*) | 1 helmsman (*kubernētēs*) |
| 54 lower oarsmen (*thalamioi*) | 1 bo'sun (*keleustēs*) |
| 14 armed men | 1 bow officer (*prōratēs*) |
| 10 citizen marines (*epibatai*) | 1 shipwright (*naupēgos*) |
| 4 Scythian archers (*toxótai*) | 1 double-pipe player (*aulētēs*) |
| | 10 deck-hands |

# TECHNICAL SPECIFICATIONS

In general, the trireme was a sleek wooden oar-powered warship armed with a bronze-sheathed waterline ram (Gk. *émbolos*). Because she was designed primarily to act as a buoyant projectile for ramming enemy vessels, the trireme was very long and narrow for her length and beam, which made it as fragile as it was fast. There were, however, noticeable structural differences between the Greek (viz. Athenian) and Persian (viz. Phoenician) versions of the trireme.

## THE EVIDENCE

Besides the inadequate data concerning its true origins, for the design of a trireme we rely upon scraps of textual and archaeological evidence. For this reason alone it is inevitable that a great deal of controversy still surrounds the trireme. But certain factors are clear. A trireme was rowed at three levels with one man to each oar. A chance remark by Thucydides, in which each Corinthian oarsman of a trireme is said to have 'carried his oar, his cushion (*hypērésion*) and his oar-loop' (2.93.2) from one side of the Isthmus to the other so as to launch a sneak attack on the port of Peiraieus, proves there was one man to each oar. An earlier reference along these lines comes from Aischylos when he has the Persian messenger say 'each sailor looped his oar about its tholepin so that it fitted well' (*Pérs.* 375–76). An oar was held in place by a leather strap, sewn into a loop (Hom. *Od.* 4.782); this was the oar-loop. The oar-loop held the oar tightly against an upright, wooden peg; this was the tholepin (Gk. *skalmós*). Again, Aischylos provides further evidence for the one-man-to-an-oar hypothesis when he uses the synonym *trískalmos* (*Pérs.* 679), literally 'with three tholepins', to describe a trireme. Xerxes himself uses it in his final line as he mourns for those 'that perished in the *triskálmoisin*' (*Pérs.* 1074), the 'three-thole-pinned ships'.

After literature, archaeology provides a variety of indirect information. The surviving inventories (e.g. *IG* $2^2$ 1606.43–44, 1607.14) of the Peiraieus naval dockyards inscribed on stone and covering a number of years in the last third of the 4th century BC, provide a wealth of detailed information, in particular the length and number of the oars in the various categories. So, we learn that these oars were of two marginally different lengths, nine cubits (3.99m) and nine and a half cubits (4.2m) long (based on the 0.444m cubit), the slightly shorter oars being needed where the hull narrows at either end, towards bow and

stern, restricting the room available to the oarsmen operating there. The odd 21cm would have been taken off the inboard end of the oars, the loom, leaving the outboard oar the same length as all the others. The difference is rightly pointed out by Aristotle when he says that in the human hand 'the end finger is short rightly and the middle finger long as in the oar amidships' (*Part. an.* 687b18). The same thing is true of the oars in a British naval cutter, the shorter ones being worked where the narrowing of the hull makes it necessary, and the sailors of smaller stature work them.

The excavated remains of the Zea ship sheds (Gk. *neōsoikoi*) at Peiraieus, built for *triērēs*, give the maximum dimensions for the ships (Athenian), that is, 37m long, 3m at the hull, increasing to 5.5m at the outriggers. The draught of these ships was relatively shallow, about 1.2m. Finally there are the vase paintings, reliefs and coins which can be claimed to represent the *triērēs*, though no ship is labelled as such.

To make two rowers take up little more space than one, need not have caused any great difficulty. But it was a far more difficult problem to fit three rowers into the same or nearly the same space. Enlarging their ships the Phoenician shipwrights provided enough height and space to fit three levels of oarsmen within the hull. The Athenian trireme differed from the Phoenician original by only having the first two levels of oarsmen within the hull, the second level working on the gunwale and the first through ports lower down. This was achieved by the invention of the *parexeiresía*, the *apostis* of more recent galleys and what we call the outrigger, a frame-like structure outside the hull and running parallel with it from stem to stern, to provide a working-

*Olympias* is a full-sized, painstakingly reconstructed, floating reconstruction of an Athenian trireme of the 5th and 4th centuries BC, which was the 'state of the art' fighting ship of the period. It was built in Greece to a design worked out by John Coates (d.2010), a retired chief naval architect to the Ministry of Defence, taking into consideration historical and archaeological evidence (admittedly disparate) researched by Professor John Morrison (d.2000), president of the Trireme Trust. Though not without her shortcomings and certainly not a replica, *Olympias* has proved herself by trial under oar and sail to be seaworthy and that the three-level oared system (with an outrigger) was not only possible, but effective. (Courtesy of the Hellenic Navy)

The Phoenician ship sheds of Kition, modern Larnaka. Because of silting, the 5th century BC naval port lies 400m inland from today's shoreline. French archaeologists from Université Lyon 2 (1987–99) unearthed six slipways connected to a perpendicular back wall. This suggests a single structure with a tiled roof under which were housed several triremes. The interior was divided into parallel boxes c.38m long and 6m wide, with rows of columns running down into the sea, which formed the partitions between the slipways. (Rjdeadly/Wikimedia Commons/CC BY-SA 3.0)

Reverse of silver third-stater of Arados, dated to 380/350 BC. Phoenicia does not provide a single representation of a warship throughout the two and a half centuries following the Nineveh bas-reliefs. In the second half of the 5th century BC nautical iconography reappears; it consists almost exclusively of representations of triremes on coins. All the triremes have a row of rim-to-rim shields, a sharply pointed forefoot like the Nineveh ships, and most probably a bronze ram. (Hermann Junghans/Wikimedia Commons/CC BY-SA 3.0)

point for the third level of oars beyond the side of the true hull. The name *parexeiresía*, which is used by Thucydides (4.12.1, 7.34.5), 'along (*para*) – outside (*ex*) – rowing (*eiresía*)' describes the purpose of the structure.

Such a structure, so characteristic of Athenian naval architecture, was quite unknown in Phoenicia because, as emphasized before, the design of the Phoenician trireme allowed for the accommodation of all the oarsmen *inside* the hull. Plutarch's statement that the Persian triremes at Salamis were *katastrōmasin hypsorophous*, 'high-roofed in their decks' (*Them.* 14.2), is probably a loose reference to their high stance in the water, as seen in the Nineveh bas-reliefs. It must be remembered that the purpose of the *parexeiresia* was to produce a sort of artificial widening of the vessel's upper-works without which three oarsmen could never have been fitted into the space previously needed for two; but there would have been no need for it if the Athenian trireme had been wider and relatively low in the water. There was a refitting programme to make the Athenian triremes originally built under Themistokles, then some 15 years old and built *en masse* and in a hurry, 'broader and given a (greater) deck span' (Plut. *Kim.* 12.2), perhaps showing Phoenician influence, carried out by Kimon just prior to his amphibious operations in Ionia.

# CONSTRUCTION

Triremes were built using the shell-first method, as opposed to skeleton-first, a skill whereby the ancient shipwright essentially shapes the hull with adjoining planks. These planks were firmly joined together edge-to-edge by large numbers of closely spaced tenon tongues fitted tightly into individual mortise slots cut into the plank edges. Next, when the close-fitting seam had been made, the tenons were pegged in place. This shell-first method is brilliantly described by Homer in his quintessential sailor's story, the *Odyssey* (5.243–61).

For strength, tenons were made of a selected hardwood, most likely Turkey oak (Lat. *Quercus cerris*), a wood common in the region in antiquity, and cut with their grain end-to-end at right-angles to that of the planks. For instance, the tenons in the Ma'agan Mikha'el, Kyrenia, and Marsala shipwrecks were constructed of oak, as were those in the six planks recovered from the Athlit ram. The dowels securing the tenons were of commoner oak. In order to secure the integrity of the hull and the planks, the joints had to be a very tight fit, and there were possibly more than 20,000 of them in a trireme, rather reminiscent of Hesiod's 'experience of many-pegged (*polygómphōn*) ships' (*Op.* 660).

The *Odyssey* underlines the importance of these closely spaced joints. When Odysseus, who alone remains of the contingent that he had led to Troy from Ithaka, was caught out in a storm after leaving Kalypso in the boat he had made for himself, he was confident that 'as long as the planks are held fast in the mortise-and-tenon joints (*harmoniai*) so long will I stay aboard and suffer the worse that comes' (*Od.* 5.361–62). The mortises were probably made by drilling, finished by chisel, and the tenons hammered home. The next plank was then carefully marked and mortised correspondingly, to fit over the protruding tenon and driven home to make a close seam. Finally, each tenon was locked firmly in place by a pair of dowels. Holes were drilled for the dowels through the planks and tenons, the dowels hammered into place from the inside of the plank. For the shell-first method of shipbuilding, Homer names the relevant tools, 'a great axe … a well-finished adze … an auger' (*Od.* 234, 237, 247). An adze, an ancient and versatile axe-like tool with its blade perpendicular

*Olympias* continues to undergo sea trials with the Hellenic Navy, into which she was commissioned as an active warship in 1987. The first specialised warship of antiquity, in its heyday the trireme offered the best naval technology had to offer. (Courtesy of the Hellenic Navy)

The Marsala Punic ship (Marsala, Museo Archeologico Regionale Baglio Anselmi) was long (35m) and slender (4.8m) and fast, powered as she was by 17 oars to each side with two men per oar. A liburnian monoreme, she went down with 49 other luckless Punic ships (Polyb. 1.61.6) on 10 March 241 BC off the Aegates Islands (Isola Egadi), a battle that was to end the First Punic War. In addition to the ship's stern, a good part of the keel and timbers from the hull port side up to the waterline were recovered. Built shellfirst using pegged mortise-and-tenon joints, the hull planking was of pine, while the keel was of elm. The tenons and dowels were of oak. (sarah_c_murray/Wikimedia Commons/CC BY-SA 2.0)

Kyrenia ship (Kyrenia, Ancient Ship Museum) discovered in November 1965 during a storm, and salvaged 1967–69. Seventy-five per cent of the timber of the ancient wreck's hull (all of Aegean pine) had been retrieved and preserved, including the whole of the keel, stem, frames and planking (3.7cm thick) to above the waterline. Though a round-bilged merchantman, a sailing vessel designed for duties entirely different from those of a trireme, both were constructed by a very specific shipbuilding technology known today as the shell-first method. The assembly of the hull planking was achieved through an intricate method of pegged mortise-and-tenons joinery, while the frames were secured with bronze spikes driven through pine dowels. Contrary to the traditional shipbuilding method, the light frames of the ancient ship were not fastened to the keel: fastened to the planking shell, the frames act as buttresses to the action of the sea. (Mgiganteus 1/ Wikimedia Commons/ CC BY-SA 3.0)

to the handle rather than parallel, was used for shaping and dressing wood. An auger was a tool for boring holes in wood.

With the skeleton-first method the framework was the primary structure, whereas with the shell-first tradition transverse framing was fitted as the shell was built up from the keel. The keel was the first and foremost important element of a trireme's construction. In order for the vessel to achieve its intended performance ability, the keel needed to be hewn correctly to receive and support shell planking, wales, and frames. Framing was secured to the shell planking by copper spikes, which had tapered square shanks and large shallow-domed heads. These spikes were driven up pine dowels previously driven up holes bored through plank and framing. The points of the spikes were clenched over and driven back into the face of the framing.

In the epic poem written in the 3rd century BC by Apollonios Rhodios, there is a description of the building of the *Argo*, believed by the author (and other ancient writers) to have been the greatest, though not the first, oared ship that had gone out on a high-sea voyage. The *Argo* was traditionally a *pentēkóntoros*. Here, the author says the Argonauts:

> First of all, by command of Argos [the shipwright], they strongly girded the ship with a rope well twisted within, stretching it tight on each side, in order that the planks might be well compacted by the tenons [*gómphoi*] and might withstand the opposing forces of the [sea] surge. (Ap. Rhod. *Argon.* 1.367–69)

Though the edge-joined construction with tongues pegged into slots made for a strong light hull, no wooden hull of the length, narrowness and fragility of the trireme could hold together when heading perpendicularly into the waves without some further support. Great stresses are placed on a seagoing hull, causing it to droop in the middle (sagging) when the crests are at the ship's extremities, or drop at both ends (hogging) when the ship is supported amidships by a single wave. This was the phenomena caused by Apollonios Rhodios' reference to 'the opposing forces of the surge'. Being a Rhodian, Apollonios knew what he was talking about. In a similar vein, Aischylos, a Salamis veteran, talks of a 'timbered ship, girded with flaxen cordage to withstand the sea' (*Supp.* 134–35).

So, to strengthen a hull made in this way the Greeks used devices called 'undergirdles' (*hypozōmata*). These were probably heavy ropes fitted low down in the ship and stretched by means of windlasses from stem to stern. In the Athenian naval inventories four are the norm for each trireme, while six are taken on distant missions (*IG* 2² 1629.11). In fact, when a trireme was in commission, she was often described as

*Kyrenia II*, launched in June 1984 and now on display at the Thalassa Municipal Museum, Agia Napa, Cyprus. During 1984 and 1985 she had numerous short sea trials in the Saronic Gulf, and then in 1986 and 1987 she took two long voyages to Cyprus. She is a faithful replica of the 4th-century BC Greek coaster found in 1967 on the seabed in the approaches to the port of Kyrenia, Cyprus. (Claus Ableiter/Wikimedia Commons/CC BY-SA 3.0)

'girded', that is to say, with the *hypozōmata* fitted (*IG 2²* 1627.29). An earlier Athenian inscription (*IG 1³* 153), dating to around 440 BC, gives a decree prescribing the minimum number of men (probably 50) allowed to rig a *hypozōma*. It is clear that considerable tension was required.

# NAVAL TIMBER

In the Old Testament, Ezekiel's famous prophecy concerns a lament for the Phoenician city of Tyre (today Sūr in Lebanon) under the similitude of a majestic seagoing ship:

> [Your builders] made your timbers of pine trees from Senir; they took cedar from Lebanon to make a mast for you. Of oaks from Bashan they made your oars; of cypress wood from the coast of Cyprus they made your deck, inlaid with ivory [possibly referring to 'lattice-' or 'trellis-work']. Fine embroidered [or sewn] linen from Egypt was your sail and served as your banner; your awnings were of blue and purple from the coasts of Elishah. Men of Sidon and Arvad [Arwad] were your oarsmen; your skilled men [e.g. pilot, or helmsman], O Tyre, were aboard as your seamen. Veteran craftsmen of Gebal [Jbeil] were on board as shipwrights to caulk your seams [presumably this ship is shell-first built]. All the ships of the sea and their sailors came alongside to trade for your wares.

Men of Persia, Lydia and Put [Libya] served as soldiers in your army. They hung their shields and helmets on your walls, bringing you splendour. (Ezek. 27:4–10 NIV)

Two important points come to the fore. First, she is a warship not a merchantman, for the Persian, Lydian and Libyan marines serving aboard hang their shields and helmets about her bulwarks. Second, the given ethnicity of these marines strongly suggest she is in the service of the Achaemenid navy.

Regarding the wood used, Ezekiel did not just list a number of different types of timber at random, but specified in detail what the various types of wood were employed for and these certainly were fitting for the ship's structures they were used for. Take, for instance, cedar and cypress. Because of its height, durability and elasticity – it needs to support the weight of the yard as well as the sail that is suspended from it without bending or snapping – cedar is the ideal timber for the mainmast. Being a tall narrow tree, cypress and its long, narrow planks are imminently suitable for decks of all types of ships. Additionally, cypress wood is also strong, has elasticity and toughness, and is lightweight and extremely durable under wet and hot conditions. In other words, the warships of Tyre were constructed using the best timber from the region, namely the forests of Cilicia, Syria and Phoenicia, though places like Mount Hermon (2,814m) are now almost bare of trees.

In the Old Testament there are splendid descriptions of the cedars of Lebanon, and the Phoenician cities which exploited the Lebanon forests played an important part in Mediterranean maritime history. The best cedar forests were almost certainly on the west slopes of Lebanon, which received more rain. This brings us to the important botanical writings of Theophrastos, a pupil of and successor to Aristotle (both were masters of classification) in the Peripatetic school. He reports that in his day the 'people of Syria and Phoenicia use Syrian cedar (*kédros*), since they cannot obtain much mountain pine (*peúkē*)' (*Hist. pl.* 5.7.1), which implies cedar was not regarded elsewhere as ship-timber in the late 4th century BC.

As types of timber used in Athenian triremes are nowadays difficult to obtain in the eastern Mediterranean, for *Olympias* it was decided to use Douglas fir (*Pseudotsuga menziesii*), whose natural home is western America and is otherwise known as Oregon pine, for the planks, as being the nearest equivalent to silver fir. The same species (instead of silver fir) was also employed for the oars in the first sea trial. This raised a problem, however, as it is not a true fir but a somewhat heavier wood, which made rowing more difficult, and for the third sea trial spruce was employed. For the tenons American live oak (*Quercus virginiana*) was used, which was akin to the Mediterranean Turkey oak (*Quercus cerris*) most likely used in ancient tenons, and for the keel, ram timbers, stem and stern, iroko (*Chlorophera excelsa*), a straight-grained hardwood from the west coast of tropical Africa. The keel (seen here) is the backbone of a ship. In order to fit the oar crew a trireme hull needs to be parallel between keel and top deck, that is, the keel has to be straight with a sharp rise aft. (© Nic Fields)

Obviously, the trireme was no 'heart of oak'. Speed required lightness and oak, though long lasting, is heavy. For lightness combined with strength, ship-timber was mostly of softwoods such as pine and fir. Plato, who deplored the effects of a maritime economy on a state's life and wrote his myth of Atlantis (mentioned in his Socratic dialogues *Timaios* and *Kritias*) as an allegory on the evils of maritime 'mobocracy' and empire, makes the Athenian stranger ask a question natural to an Athenian: 'How is the environment of our colonial city off for ship-timber?' He gets the answer:

> There is no silver fir (*elátē*) to speak of, nor mountain pine (*peúkē*), and but little cypress (*kypárissos*); nor could one find much coastal pine (*pítus*) or plane (*plátanos*), which shipwrights are always obliged to use for the interior fittings of ships (*tōn ploíōn*). (Pl. *Leg.* 4.705c)

Plato does not specify what sort of ships he is referring to, but Theophrastos, a younger contemporary of Plato, lists the three principle timbers for trireme construction as silver fir (*elátē*), mountain pine (*peúkē*), and Syrian cedar (*kédros*):

The deck and gangway on *Olympias*. Unlike that on a Phoenician trireme, with its complete deck and surrounding bulwark, on an Athenian trireme the deck was a flimsy affair, a narrow wooden canopy open in the centre for a gangway that ran from the quarterdeck to bow. There was no deck rail.
[© Nic Fields]

> [F]or triremes and long ships [i.e. other warships] are made of silver fir, because of its lightness, and merchant ships of mountain pine, because it does not decay; while some make triremes of it because they are ill-provided with silver fir. (Theophr. *Hist. pl.* 5.7.1, cf. Ar. *Eq.* 1310, Hom. *Il.* 13.389–91, 16.482–84)

Thanks mainly to Theophrastos, we know a good deal regarding the type of timber the Greeks used in shipbuilding. Earlier in the same treatise, he notes that silver fir 'also gives timber of the greatest lengths and of the straightest growth; wherefore yardarms and masts are made from it' (*Hist. pl.* 5.1.7). Likewise, the elder Pliny (*HN* 16.195) says that silver fir is preferred for these items of gear because of its light weight. Native to the mountains of Europe and rarely found below 800m, the silver fir (Lat. *Abies alba*: in Virgil [*Aen.* 5.663, 8.91] *abies* is accepted as a poetic name for a trireme) can grow to 40–50m tall and with a trunk diameter up to 1.5m. When grown in high forest conditions where the trees are closer together and compete for light, the natural result is longer lengths of straight timber, which provided sail yards and masts in usually a single piece. In such conditions the silver fir also sheds its lower branches and is therefore more free from knots.

In central and southern Greece the silver fir grew on most of the mountains that were more than 1,000m high, but it was a different variety, *Abies cephalonica*, which was generally regarded as inferior in quality, Theophrastos (*Hist. pl.* 5.2.1) ranking the timber of Parnassus, for instance, well below that of Macedonia.

Growing at lower altitudes, the mountain pine comes in two varieties, *Pinus larico* and *Pinus nigra*, the latter belonging to Greece and the eastern Mediterranean. It was these mountain pines that were the most used in shipbuilding. As for wood for the internal structure, Theophrastos has this to say:

> For triremes some make such parts of Aleppo pine (*peúkē*) because of its lightness.

The cutwater, to which the sheathing is attached, and the catheads are made of ash (*melía*), mulberry (*sukáminos*), or elm (*pteléā*); for these parts must be strong. (Theophr. *Hist. pl.* 5.7.3)

Silver double-shekel (Paris, Bibliothèque nationale de France) of `Abd`aštart I of Sidon (r. 365–352 BC). On the obverse, a Sidonian trireme (note the stepping of the oars); on the reverse, the Great King in his chariot followed behind by the Sidonian king who holds a sceptre and a votive vase (imagery reflects Sidon's formal submission to Achaemenid rule). (Gallica Digital Library, BnF/CC-1 [1])

Aleppo pine (Lat. *Pinus halepensis*) was the most widespread of the Mediterranean pines generally found at low altitudes and particularly by the coasts. Nowadays the resin of the Aleppo pine is used to flavour Retsina. Elm (Lat. *Ulmus minor*), on the other hand, was noted particularly for its strength and resistance to shock. A stem fragment of elm was recovered from the interior of the Egadi 10 ram, a mid-3rd-century BC bronze-sheathed, three-fined waterline ram, and the chock and the nosing found inside the Athlit ram were of elm as well.

# TROUBLESHOOTING

Let us begin with the obvious: the emphasis on lightness for the timber for the hull and for the rest of a trireme was a prime consideration in its overall design. Although we do not know the name of a single trireme that fought at Salamis, for instance, we do have hundreds of such names surviving from 4th-century BC Athens: one such Athenian trireme was called by the name *Kouphotatē* – 'Lightness' (*IG* 2² 1629.1).

One result of using softwoods to achieve the necessary lightness was that the hull of a trireme tended to soak up water. Theophrastos, admittedly referring to doors made of silver fir and not hulls, says they were stood up but not finished until the following year, 'for in summer the wood dries and the boards come apart, but in the winter they come together again' (*Hist. pl.* 5.3.5). The reason, he says, is that the open fleshy texture of the wood of the silver fir absorbs the moisture in the air. Consequently, all triremes were beached and manhandled out of the water as often as possible so as to dry and clean the hulls, which the Hellenic League fleet was unable to do before the battle of Salamis. Something similar would happen to the Athenian triremes 67 years later in 413 BC during another crucial trireme battle. One of the most serious problems for the Athenians besieging Syracuse by land and sea was the enemy had the luxury to launch their ships at any time they chose, whereas the Athenians, having no reserve of vessels, had to keep all theirs constantly in the water in case of sudden attack. As a result, their hulls had become waterlogged and fouled, and they could not make anything like their maximum speed (Thuc. 7.12.3–5).

As mentioned previously, the hulls would not only become waterlogged and leaky, but worse still they would suffer from that scourge of wooden ships, the naval borer (Gk. *terēdōn*, Lat. *teredo navalis*), which is the maritime equivalent of woodworm or death-watch beetle. Naval shipworm attack was by far and away the greatest menace to the viability of the trireme as a weapon. In Aristophanes' comedy *Equites* (1300–15), written in 424 BC, the triremes had assembled to discuss their concerns about the plans of Hyperbolos, the leading demagogue of the day, to send an armada of 100 ships against Carthage:

> All were indignant, and one of them, as yet a virgin, cried 'May god forbid that I should ever obey him! I would prefer to grow old in the harbour and be gnawed by worms. No! By the gods I swear it. Nauphante, daughter of Nauson, shall never bend to his law; that's as true as I am made of mountain pine (*ek peúkēs*) and joinery (*kài xúlōn*)²...'
>
> (Ar. *Eq.* 1305–10)

In the spring of 1995, the planking of the full-sized reconstruction *Olympias* was found to be damaged by *terēdōn*, so much so that extensive re-planking was necessary to make the vessel operational (Rankov 2012: 203).

Once fastened to a submerged wooden surface, the *terēdōn* quickly bores a hole by wielding the razor-like edge of its vestigial shell as a rasp. From this wooden sanctuary the bivalve mollusc will never emerge (the misleading term 'shipworm' is common because of the worm-like elongation of its body). Once ensconced in the hole, the sharp shell at the anterior end of the worm-like body continues to burrow deeper. The pulverized wood serves as food. As the burrow extends into the timber little by little, the remorseless mollusc grows to fill its ever-extending home. Within a month the *terēdōn* can reach 30cm in length (depending on the species and the environment, the family *Teredinidae* can reach a length of up to 45cm and a diameter

---

2   Following the Budé translator who correctly gives *bois charpenté* for *xúlōn*.

of about 1.5cm). Now it is ready to eject swarms of its own larvae into the sea, starting a new cycle. A single adult produces several generations and millions of larvae within one year (the *terēdōn* is a hermaphrodite), and it usually has a lifespan of two to three years. Ancient shipwrights avoided using certain woods for the hull because they were thought to be susceptible to it, larch (viz. coastal pine) particularly so according to the elder Pliny (*HN* 16.79), while Theophrastos points out 'that the wood of the mountain pine is more likely to be eaten by the *terēdōn* than that of the silver fir' (*Hist. pl.* 5.4.4).

# SUPPLY

These woods were not plentiful at all times in Greece, and for shipbuilding timber Athens had to look outside its own borders. As the Old Oligarch grumbles, 'no one *polis* has both timber and flax [viz. for shipbuilding], but where flax is common the land is level and treeless' (Xen. [*Ath. pol.*] 2.12), that is, the plains have been cleared for agriculture; food crops being more important than timber trees. The Old Oligarch was always keen to look for any weaknesses in the 'trireme democracy' of Athens, but even so he had a point, for the Athenians had to import large quantities of timber felled and sawed mainly from the well-forested mountains of Macedonia and Thrace (Xen. *Hell.* 6.1.11).

A string of treaties with Macedonian kings guaranteed Athens' right to import high quality timber from Macedon or to send its shipwrights there to build ships on the spot so saving the costly transport by sea (*IG* 1³ 89, 117, 182). But since supplies depended on friendly relations with the Macedonian kings, and Macedonian kings were rarely secure on their thrones, Athens must from time to time have been forced to turn elsewhere. Italy was another good source for suitable shipbuilding timber. Speaking of the aforementioned Syracusan shipbuilding programme of 399 BC, namely that of the tyrant Dionysios I, Diodorus Siculus mentions the procurement from Italy 'of both excellent silver fir (*elátē*) and mountain pine (*peúkē*)' (14.41.4).

It goes without saying that oars (Gk. *kōpai*) were a vital part of a trireme's gear, and it was obviously important to ensure that a vessel was not handicapped by weak or damaged oars. In Homer 'shaved fir' (*Il.* 7.5, *Od.* 12.172) is a synonym for oars, and each oar-shaft was made from a rough, young silver fir, very carefully prepared (Theophr. *Hist. pl.* 5.1.7). Stripping coaxial layers from saplings ensured the grain of the wood was aligned along the shaft, making the oars strong for their weight. The Athenian naval inventories show how carefully the oars were inspected for faults and those that were sub-standard were rejected (*IG* 2² 1604.34, 1604.35, 1604.53–54); inscribed on stone tablets, these prosaic records are lucid, official and unequivocal.

The procurement of suitable oar-timber was important to Athens. Thrace, in which Athens had a continuing interest throughout the period of its naval ascendancy, is noted by Herodotos as having 'abundant forests for shipbuilding, much wood for oars, mines of silver' (5.23.2). Perdikkas II, the king of Macedon

(r. 448–413 BC), signed a treaty with Athens, probably during the Peloponnesian War, engaging himself to export Macedonian oar timber, at the discount price of five drachmae apiece, to Athens alone (*IG* 1³ 89.31). A catalogue of the extraordinary variety of goods imported into Athens by sea in a comedy written by the one-eyed Hermippos and performed in 425 BC, or thereabouts, has an interesting entry denouncing Perdikkas of Macedon as a notorious liar: 'And from

Perdikkas lies with very many ships' (fr. 63.8 *Phormophoroi* apud Ath. 1.27e–28a), which reminds his Athenian audience not only of 'lies by the boatload' but also of readymade ships being imported from Macedonia. Thucydides, reporting the events leading up to the Peloponnesian War, says the king 'had from an old friend and ally been made an enemy' (1.57.2); indeed, as the war progressed, Perdikkas was to prove the most adamant foe and fickle ally of Athens, switching sides on numerous occasions (Thuc. 2.29.6, 4.79.2, 4.128.5, 5.83.4, 6.7.4, 7.9). He is accordingly denounced by Hermippos as a notorious liar, rather than as a shrewd political survivor who sided with Athens when it suited him, as a more objective observer might have put it. As timber was a royal monopoly in the kingdom, Perdikkas was a constant threat to Athenian interests in the region. A fragmentary inscription, perhaps honouring Perdikkas' son and successor Archelaos I (r. 413–399 BC), also survives mentioning oar-spars (Fornara 161.30).

The most common epithet for ships in Homer after 'swift' is 'black', the blackness being the result of applications of pine pitch on ships' hulls to make them watertight. The same is true of Athenian triremes. Aristophanes, in his comedy the *Acharnians*, has an envoy return from Sparta armed with a five-year truce, but the local hero Dikaiopolis, who is keen to end the war, does not like it because 'it smells of pitch and naval preparations' (190). Ships preparing for an expedition were given a coat of pitch. The substance is mentioned in one of the naval inventories (*IG* 2² 1622.740, cf. 1627.313), where it is listed as part of the gear for a trireme, *Amphitrite*, which suggests it was carried aboard for use when the vessel was hauled up ashore for on the spot maintenance.

Once at Peiraieus, naval supplies were protected by an export ban. We only know, from a casual remark from Aristophanes (*Ran.* 364), of a prohibition on the shipment overseas of the leather tubular sleeves (*askōmata*), which kept water slopping through the lower oar ports, sailcloth and pitch, but restrictions of this kind would have applied to all other nautical items such as ropes. In the aforementioned *Phormophoroi* (literally 'Basketbearers', the stevedores who

One of the objectives regarding *Olympias* was to discover her true performance at sea, both under oar and under sail. A propos the latter, she was sailed at least four short periods during each season of sea trials around the island of Poros, and in 1992 she sailed for a full day, before the wind, from Salamis, east of Aegina, to Poros. The results were impressive, in particular her ability to sail close to the wind with minimal leeway. The main mast is stepped about amidships, whilst a second, the 'boat' mast, is raked and stepped forward. Ancient sails were either of papyrus ('light') or of flax ('heavy'), as were ropes. Sails were used for propulsion when the vessel was not engaged in battle. *Olympias* has given good indications of being very close to the original Athenian trireme. Of course, there are those who would dispute this, particularly with regards to the number of banks, levels and oarsmen; so much dissent and disagreement, factionalism and feuding has enlivened the trireme debate. (Courtesy of the Hellenic Navy)

31

Bronze-sheathed trireme ram (Peiraieus, Hellenic Maritime Museum), a copy of which was fixed to *Olympias*. It weighs some 200kg. (Mariegriffiths/Wikimedia Commons/CC BY-SA 3.0)

**BELOW**

In November 1980 an intact warship waterline ram was found on the seabed off the coast near Athlit just south of Haifa, with 16 hull timbers encased in it. These timbers show the same method of construction as the Kyrenia ship. The ram (held at Haifa, Israeli National Maritime Museum) is a hefty 600kg of hardwood and high-quality, single-cast bronze. (Oren Rozen/Wikimedia Commons/CC BY-SA 3.0)

**BELOW RIGHT**

The ram is decorated with symbols: Poseidon's trident; eagle's head; wreathed pilos helmet surmounted by eight-pointed star (sign of the Dioskouri); caduceus bound with fillet (wand of Hermes). All four symbols are found together on coins minted on Cyprus during the reign of Ptolemaios V Epiphanes (r. 209–181 BC). (Oren Rozen/Wikimedia Commons/CC BY-SA 3.0)

unloaded the merchantmen), Hermippos says 'the hanging gear' (fr. 63.12 apud Ath. 1.27e–28a) was imported from Egypt, that is to say, linen sailcloth and papyrus ropes.

# ARMAMENT

The primary weapon of a trireme was the bronze-sheathed waterline ram (Gk. *embólos*) situated at the prow. Aischylos speaks of the use of 'brazen rams' (*Pérs.* 408, 415) at Salamis, and they appear in the Athenian naval inventories as returnable items when a ship is broken up (*IG* 2² 1623.113–23, 1628.498, cf. 1629.813–16).

The waterline ram, made more destructive by placing a tightly fitting bronze sheath over the projecting part of the keel, delivered a pounding blow, splitting the seam of the opposing ship. Analysis of the timbers preserved inside Athlit ram has provided a fascinating glimpse into how a waterline ram was carefully designed and constructed to deliver the blow of its ship as it absorbed and transferred the shock of the ramming manoeuvre to the structural timbers of the ship's light hull. This was achieved by the merging of the keel, bottom planks and wales running the whole length of the ship into the ramming timber (Casson and Steffy 1991: 6–39). The size and strength of these timbers formed, in the words of Richard Steffy, a renowned specialist on ancient shipbuilding, 'a giant arrow'.

Not only did the trireme bear witness to the very high level of craftsmanship in wood, it was also an example of contemporary engineering at its highest order. A complex solid bronze casting, a ram was produced either by the 'lost wax' process, or poured into a sand mould with a central core in one operation. The Athenians preferred a ram with its business end flared into three horizontal narrow fins, rather than the tip coming to a point, in order to prevent it from getting wedged in the hull of its opponent. Were this to occur, it could have spelled disaster for the attacking vessel, locking her into a deadly embrace that would allow other enemy triremes to ram the erstwhile attacker. Instead, according to Steffy, the three-fined fin ram was designed to open the planking seams which were held together by the tightly fitting pegged mortise-and-tenon joinery. Once ruptured, the oak tenons would have held the seams open, permitting seawater to pour into the hull of the victim. Oddly enough, it appears from the iconographical evidence, admittedly meagre, that in our period of study the Phoenicians still employed the conically shaped ram ending in a sharp point.

Ramming itself required great skill, for the opponent's hull had to be hit with enough force to cause significant damage but not so much as to entangle the attacking vessel in the splintered hull, preventing the oarsmen from backing their ship away to safety. Impact theory indicates that the speed of the attacker need be only 3–4kn at an angle of attack between 20° and 70° (measured midline to midline) if the target vessel was either stationary or moving towards the attacker, while a speed of 2–3kn is sufficient when the target vessel was struck amidships. Lower speeds meant at the moment of impact, the ram would crumple, while the target vessel escaped almost unscathed.

The bow of *Olympias* showing the bronze-sheathed ram and the box-like *epōtides* – literary 'ear-timbers' – or catheads, which protect the outriggers from being sheered off. A ram like this was capable of smashing a hole in a ship's side at its waterline. But a ship holed in this manner, though crippled, would not sink (Gk. *katadúein*, literally 'to dip') when flooded – triremes carried little or nothing in the way of ballast or stores – but when completely bilged would lie waterlogged in the water (flooded and capsized hulls would be towed off as booty). In such a state a ship was likely to have lolled on to one outrigger the other, so making it *hors de combat*. (© Nic Fields)

33

# BRONZE-SHEATHED WATERLINE RAMS

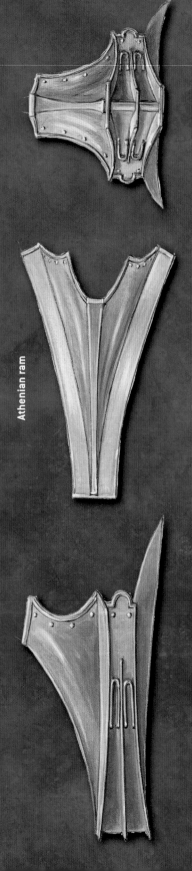

Athenian ram

Phoenician ram

The main weapon of a trireme was the bronze-sheathed waterline ram situated at the prow. In an Athenian trireme, the ram was formed by the forward tip of the keel, heavily armoured and built up to a point just above the waterline. The timbers had to be heavy enough and the casting thick enough to endure repeated collisions. The three-finned design reduced the risk of embedding during the blow.

The Phoenicians, on the other hand, still favoured a long, conical ram positioned just under the waterline, though it too was armoured in bronze.

# THE COMBATANTS

A triremes was a complicated oared warship in which a maximum number of men was packed into a minimum space; in 480 BC the full complement (Gk. *plērōma*) of a trireme, whether Greek or Persian, was 200 (Hdt. 3.13.1–2, 7.184.1, 7.185.1, 8.17, cf. Thuc. 6.8, 8.29.2, Xen. *Hell.* 1.5.3–7), of whom 170 were the oarsmen (Gk. *eretai*) needed to propel the vessel. Every Persian ship was supplied by a Persian subject state, eastern Mediterranean peoples such as the Phoenicians, Egyptians, Karians, Cypriots and Greeks from the eastern Aegean, among others.

It is worth making two points at this juncture: first, as many Greeks fought for the Great King as against him; and second, in truth there was not one Persian trireme in Xerxes' grand armada. The non-seafaring Persians supplied only admirals and marines. This should not come as a surprise. The Achaemenid Persian empire, after all, was won by land and remained land-centred, and so the strength of the empire lay in the army, of which the mainstay was the foot soldier.

## OARSMEN

In Athens the oarsmen (*naūtai*) were not slaves but highly trained professionals, fit hard men drawn from the fourth property class as defined by the constitution of the lawgiver Solon (*fl.* 595 BC), the *thētes*. These were the poorest Athenian citizens, what Aristotle called 'the trireme democracy' (*Pol.* 1291b21) or, in the more memorable phrase of his, *naūtikòs ochlos*, the 'naval mob' (*Pol.* 1327b37, cf. Thuc. 8.72.2). They were renowned for their skills as seamen by Thucydides (1.80.4), himself a *triērarchos*, it will be recalled, and knew what he was talking about. Of the

# ATHENIAN STRATĒGOI

According to the testimony of the author of the Ἀθηναίων πολιτεία (61.1, cf. 22.5) from 487/486 BC onwards ten stratēgoi ('generals'), the former tribal commanders, were now annually elected (not chosen by lot) by the citizens of Athens. Unlike other Athenian magistrates, stratēgoi could be re-elected as long as they held the confidence of the dēmos, and in this way they might exercise great personal influence and ensure an all-important continuity of policy. As a consequence, a generalship quite quickly became the principal political prize for an ambitious Athenian. More importantly, the position itself took on executive duties that were more than merely military in nature. As such, the generals' responsibilities were those of domestic and foreign policy subject to the control of the ekklēsía. Fortifications and munitions, both military and naval armaments, mustering of citizen soldiers and citizen oarsmen and the imposition of war taxes all fell within the scope of their administration. Athenian stratēgoi, of course, could be appointed as commanders both in the field and at sea (unlike the Spartans, the Athenians lacked a specific word for 'admiral'), taking responsibility for strategic and – up to a point – tactical decisions.

The ruinous campaign against Syracuse which Athens embarked on in 415 BC witnessed the defection of one of its stratēgoi, the death of another and the illness of a third. Shown here is Porto Grande di Siracusa, looking towards the harbour entrance, where the final sea battle took place, involving some 200 fully laden triremes. (© Esther Carré)

thētes, according to the pamphleteer known as the 'Old Oligarch', 'the majority can row as soon as they get aboard since they have practised throughout their lives' (Xen. [Ath. pol.] 1.20). This is a view that accords well with the words Thucydides puts into the mouth of the Athenian statesman Perikles (d.429 BC): namely 'seapower is a matter of skill (téchnēs) … and it is not possible to get practice in the odd moment when the chance occurs, but is a full-time occupation, leaving no moment for other things' (1.142.9). Just as competition rowers do today, the oarsmen of antiquity employed a co-ordinated stroke. At Salamis Aischylos eloquently speaks of the Greek oarsmen, 'with the even stroke of foaming oars, they smote the briny deep' (kōpēs … xynembolē, Pérs. 396–97). As the Old Oligarch implies, it is most likely that oar crews, at least in Athens, were made up of men who had already gained experience in smaller ships and boats.

According to the comprehensive lists of naval stores held in the Athenian arsenal of the 4th century BC, there were 27 oarsmen each side at the lowest level of the trireme, the thalamioi, or hold-rowers. These men worked their oars through oar ports, thalamia, which was an easy rowing position much akin to that of a Thames skiff.[3] In the middle level seated on the hull's crossbeams or thwarts, zuga, there were

---

3   The oars of a Thames skiff are likewise held in place by tholepins, and the thwart, or seat, is fixed.

27 oarsmen each side, the *zugioi*, or thwart-rowers, which meant their oars were in the natural position (these were the original oarsmen of a single-banked ship). The top level of oarsmen, the *thranitai*, or stool-rowers, 31 on each side, rowed through an outrigger, *parexeiresía*. This was an extension beyond the side of the trireme, which gave greater leverage to the oars. The other advantage in this arrangement was the *thranitai* were to one side ('outboard') of those below them, which meant they did not have to be so far above them vertically. This lowered the centre of gravity, making the trireme more stable without increasing its beam. Also, it enabled them to use oars of the same length as those of the other two levels, without having to hold them at a very steep angle to the water. Even so, their task was considered the hardest.

Whether or not those who pulled an oar at Salamis were paid, we have no way of knowing. Though the author of Ἀθηναίων πολιτεία (Arist. [*Ath. pol.*] 23.1) claims, which is repeated by Plutarch (*Them.* 10.4, cf. *Kim.* 9.4), the Aeropagos provided each fighting man with an allowance of eight drachmae just prior to Salamis, the Decree of Themistokles makes no mention of it. But when rates of naval pay are recorded, the *thranitai*, who as leaders of a 'triad' had a greater responsibility for synchronized rowing since they were in the unique position to see both the oar blades enter the water and the inside of the vessel, were provided with bonuses on top of their daily wage. According to Thucydides 'the crews of the ships were all paid at the same rate' (3.17.4); before 413 BC this rate was paid at a drachma a day (6.31.3, cf. 6.8.1), which meant it cost about one talent per month to operate one trireme; he also records that the *thranitai* received extra pay (6.31.3). Only half the rate of a drachma a day was actually payable to Athenian crews while on active service; the rest

*Thranitai* stations on *Olympias*. Each station has a width of 49cm according to the two-cubit *interscalium* provided by the Roman architect Vitruvius (1.2.4), which marked the distance between tholepins in an oared ship. This lack of space for movement poses a major problem for modern varsity rowers. To obtain the best performance a rower should be able to reach forward with his/her arm straight at each catch, and move from the hips, using additional force from the leg muscles, which is greatly helped by a rolling seat. But on *Olympias* the seats are fixed, and the total horizontal movement of the rower's hands is limited to about 85cm. This means that any rower more than about 1.72m tall cannot straighten his/her arms at the catch without hitting the back of the rower in front. So instead of relaxing his/her arm muscles, the rower has to waste energy in keeping them taut. (© Nic Fields)

# DECREE OF THEMISTOKLES

Known from the name of the politician who moved its passage in the *ekklēsía*, the decree was the official state record of the provisions for meeting the expected Persian invasion led by Xerxes. Themistokles' proposal was that the Athenians and all foreigners (*métoikoi*) who reside in Athens should send their women and children to Troizen. All able-bodied men of fighting age should then embark on the 200 triremes that have been prepared to fight the 'long-haired Medes'. Finally, the Athenians who had been ostracized were recalled. An extract from the inscription is provided below:

The *stratēgoi* are to appoint, starting tomorrow, 200 *triērarchoi*, one to a ship, from among those who have land and house in Athens and legitimate children and who are not older than 50; to these men the ships are to be assigned by lot. They are to enlist marines [*epibátai*, literally 'deck soldiers' i.e. hoplites], ten to each ship, from men between the ages of 20 and 30, and four archers. They are to distribute the servicemen by lot at the same time as they assign the *triērarchoi* to the ships by lot. The *stratēgoi* are to write up the rest, ship by ship, on white boards, [taking] the Athenians from the lexiarchic registers and the foreigners from those registered with the *polémarchos*. They are to write them up assigning them by divisions, 200 of about 100 (men) each, and to write above each division the name of the trireme and of the *triērarchos* and the servicemen, so that they may know on which trireme each division is to embark … When the ships have been manned, with 100 of them they are to meet the enemy at Artemision in Euboia, and with the other 100 they are to lie off Salamis and the coast of Attica and keep guard over the land. [Fornara 55]

Decree of Themistokles (Athens, Epigraphical Museum, inv. EM 13330) inscribed upon a marble stele, dated to the first half of the 3rd century BC. The text is cut in the classical manner, *stoichēdon*, each letter below a letter of the preceding line, with 42 letters to a line. Although inscribed with 3rd-century BC lettering, some scholars believe it to be a later patriotic fabrication, rather than a true copy of an official Athenian decree of 481/480 BC. (Marsyas/Wikimedia Commons/CC BY-SA 3.0)

became due when the ship was paid off in Peiraieus (Thuc. 8.45.2, Ar. *Eq.* 1366-7). Comparisons with modern money are meaningless. Suffice to say that a drachma per diem was a standard wage in Athens, such as might be earned by a skilled worker, but the difference would have been that this was a regular income and not dependent on finding employment.

The cushion or rowing pad, *hypērésion* (literally 'under the oarsman'), in our Greek texts (Thuc. 2.93.2, Eup. fr. 54 *Autolykos*, Isok. 8.48, Hermippos. fr. 34, Theophr. *Char.* 2.11) is variously defined as a fleece, a hide, or a pillow that kept the oarsman wearing out his backside (Ar. *Eq.* 784–85, 1366–68, cf. *Ran.* 236–38). It is clear that the cushion was tied to the oarsman; the Athenian orator Isokrates (8.48) grumbles about the ridiculous figure cut by his fellow Athenians when they go ashore wearing their rowing pads. Rather than simply leaning forward and backward and making use only of their upper bodies in rowing, John Hale (1996) argues that the oarsmen made use of a sliding technique in order to maximize their speed, efficiency, and manoeuvrability. Undoubtedly modern rowing is a matter of leg work, not upper body work. A noted oarsman himself, Hale postulates that the Athenians adopted a similar method of rowing where most of the power came from movement in

the oarsmen's legs: by wearing a cushion strapped to their backsides, they could slide forward (i.e. towards the stern) and backward (i.e. towards the bow) along a hardwood bench, extending their arms to push and pull for added distance. Any sliding, however, would be over a much shorter distance than in a modern racing craft, some 15cm as opposed to 40–50cm actual movement on the modern sliding seats with wheels. Nevertheless, such a technique would have certainly given the Athenian oarsmen an advantage over those whose seats were fixed. This point was first made by Hale (1973) commenting on the raised knees of two oarsmen in the Lenormant relief. There is also a line from an Attic comic play in which a novice oarsman is told to 'extend your legs' (Eup. fr. 268 *Taxiarchoi*).

Although the oarsmen were protected to a certain degree from weather and in battle from enemy missiles by the canopy deck (Gk. *katástrōma*) over their heads, the trireme was open at the sides above the topwale. At a much later date the Syracusans would exploit this weakness during the early sea battles in the Great Harbour at Syracuse (413 BC); here men in skiffs dart under the oar banks of Athenian triremes, and coming alongside throw missiles among the oarsmen (Thuc. 7.40.5). There are side screens (Gk. *pararrymáta*) of canvas and hide among the gear of triremes in the Athenian naval inventories (*IG* 2² 1605.40–43, 1609.85–87, 1609.113, 1611.244–49, 1612.73–79, 1627.348). The last were presumably for protection against such attacks, while the first were for the protection against the elements. In Xenophon (*Hell.* 2.1.22, cf. 1.6.19) vertical side screens are hung over the outriggers before battle.

Little wonder, therefore, oarsmen had no control over, and little idea of, what was happening during an engagement. True, they were to some extent insulated from the action above their heads, not only because they faced away from the enemy when attacking, but also they could not see outside their ship at all. For them, it was 'the huge din caused by the number of ships crashing together that not only spread terror, but made the *keleustaí* inaudible' (Thuc. 7.70.6).

Pentelic marble fragment (Athens, New Acropolis Museum, inv. 1339) depicting the middle section of the starboard side of an Athenian trireme under oar, known as the Lenormant relief (after its discoverer) and dated to around 410 BC. Found in 1859 near the Erechteion on the Acropolis of Athens, the shallow relief shows nine oarsmen pulling at their oars, sitting naked and facing aft (note, #7 and #9 have raised knees). The visible oarsmen are nine of the 31 *thranitai* (on one side), who sit under the shelter of a canopy deck supported by curved stanchions and whose oars work through parallel timbers of the outrigger, while two lower levels of oars emerge from the ship's side. These represent the *zugioi* on the thwarts, with the *thalamioi* below and behind them. (Marsyas/Wikimedia Commons/ CC BY-SA 2.5)

The trireme debate (featuring strong opinions) revolves around disputes between the one-levellers, two-levellers, three-levellers, the single and triple benchers (and variations thereof), which entails one wading through a thick undergrowth of controversy generated by scholars, pendants, and dilettantes. Still, the five series of sea trials (1987, 1988, 1990, 1992 and 1994) proved that a modern oar crew can comfortably operate seated on three levels and secure a peak speed of 7.1kn for a period of just under five minutes. The best-recorded measured mile was covered at 7.05kn with a flying start (Shaw 1993: 42). In Thucydides (8.95.2) an *axynkrotetos plērōma* is an oar crew not trained to pull together. So this result, achieved with inexperienced oar crews of international men and women who are mostly trained for sprinting, indicates that Thucydides (3.49) and Xenophon (6.4.2) were not exaggerating about straight-line performance with regards to a 'fast trireme' (*triērēs tachús*). When not undergoing sea trials, *Olympias* is in dry-dock and on display at the Park of Maritime Tradition in Palaió Fáliro. (Filos96/Wikimedia Commons/Public Domain)

The furniture for an oarsman: seat, foot stretcher, tholepin, and oar port. The seat has edge bolsters to prevent the occupant from sliding sideways on a roll. In antiquity, it is quite likely that oarsmen occupied regular positions within the vessel since it would have allowed them to perfect their sweeps with the same members of the crew around them, especially in the fixed vertical 'triad'. This was the case in *Olympias*. (© Nic Fields)

It must be added that of the three, the *thalamioi* had the most unpleasant and dangerous position. If the ship got badly holed, they were most likely to be drowned or captured by an enemy boarding-party before they could have made their escape. Oarsmen were unarmed. Much less of a physical danger, as Aristophanes (*Ran.* 1074) points out with rather plain vulgarity, was the fact that they sat with their faces rather too close to the backsides of the *zugioi* above and in front of them. Gliding between patriotism and satire, Aristophanes' *Ranae* features many comments on the Athenian navy.

# OARSMEN

In contrast to modern rowing vessels, a trireme had much steeper oar angles and seats which are fixed wooden benches. This meant the effort of rowing was shifted towards the arms and back, pulling the oar while bending from the waist (as shown here in the three upper illustrations) rather than with the straight, upright posture used by modern rowers. The underwater area of a trireme was about 100m² (0.6m² per ancient oarsman); a modern racing eight has twice as much water resistance to overcome at 1.2m² per rower.

In the hot and narrow space below the canopy deck, the barefooted oarsman wears little more than a loincloth. Each oar is some 4.5m in length, with a short, but wide and flat, oar blade. The handgrip at the butt is long enough for the oarsman's hands to be kept about two hands' breaths apart. The oar-loop, which lashes the oar to the tholepin, takes the whole strain of the pull. Homer (*Od.* 4.782) refers to oar-loops of leather, but experience in *Olympias* has been that leather oar-loops stretch and break. Rope grommets are better. Whatever material used, they had to be greased from time to time with mutton tallow.

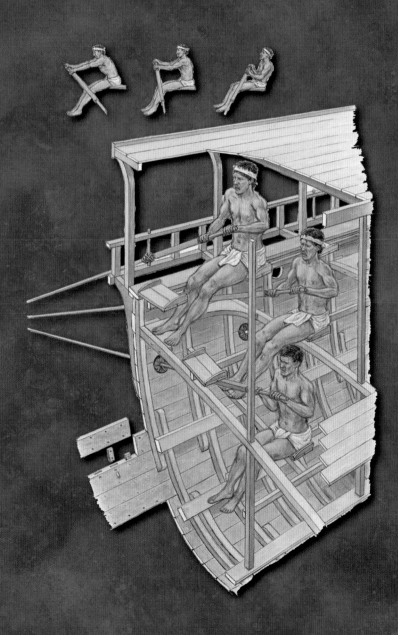

With its highly developed direct democracy, Athens esteemed its oarsmen as highly as its hoplites (e.g. Ar. *Vesp.* 1117–20, *Lys.* 7.41, 30.26), and Aristophanes' audience were intimately familiar with the ships and the sailors of the fleet. Because a good many men in his audience had rowed the triremes, the savage satirist nails it: entombed in their murky, foetid and cramped quarters, the *thalamioi* would have suffered too from the sweat of those above dripping down on them. Because of the objectionable odour, the reconstructed trireme *Olympias* 'had to be washed out with sea water at least once every four days' (Morrison, Coates and Rankov 2000: 238) to remain tolerable. Similarly, their oar ports were only about 45cm above the waterline, and even with efficient *askōmata*, the *thalamioi* must have got pretty wet. The fact that these oar ports were larger than the ones above, though obviously inconvenient, was because an increase in size was required to allow the oars of the *thalamioi*, which were pivoted nearer the centre of the trireme than those at the two higher levels, to function at all.

To sum up, the three categories of Athenian oarsmen are as follows:

| | | |
|---|---|---|
| *thranitai* | 62 upper oarsmen |
| *zugioi* | 54 middle oarsmen |
| *thalamioi* | 54 lower oarsmen |

Giving a total of 170 oarsmen (cf. Jordan 2000: 81–84, Tilley 2004: 30–31), which is exactly the number of oars, not counting the 30 spares (*kōpai perineō*), supplied to an Athenian trireme (*IG* 2² 1607.9.19). The spares were carried on board in case of breakages in the 170 working oars.

# DECK CREW

According to the Decree of Themistokles, which records the measures taken by the Athenian assembly (*ekklēsía*) in 481 BC to meet the threatened Persian invasion, the fighting men of an Athenian trireme included hoplites (*hoplítai*), enlisted as 'deck-

The Lenormant relief (along with the two other smaller fragments) originally formed part of a monument depicting the Athenian state trireme *Paralos*, seen here with her *prōratēs*, bow officer, lying propped up on one elbow at the forward end of the deck and signals aft with one hand, and the hero Paralos, inventor of navigation, at the upper right. The reconstruction is based on a drawing made for the Cavaliero dal Pozzo in Rome, now in the British Museum. (Tilemachos Efthimiadis/Wikimedia Commons/CC BY-SA 2.0)

soldiers (*epibátai*), ten for each ship, from men over 20 years of age up to 30, and archers (*toxótai*), four in number' (Fornara. 25–26). This practice appears to have continued throughout the 5th century BC (Thuc. 2.23.2, 3.94.1, 3.95.2, cf. 2.56.2, Plut. *Them* 14.2), although 4th-century BC crew-lists often give only two or three archers. One trireme, for example, had 11 *epibátai* and three *toxótai* (*IG* 2² 1951.82–84).

This left ten deckhands plus the trireme commander (*triērarchos*), the helmsman (*kubernētēs*), the bow officer (*prōratēs*), the purser (*pentēkontarchos*), who distributed pay and provisions, the shipwright (*naupēgos*), who made emergency repairs, the bo'sun (*keleustēs*, 'exhorter'), who controlled the oarsmen, and a double-pipe player (*aulētēs*), who piped time for them (Xen. [*Ath. pol.*] 1.2, *IG* 2² 1951.94–105). Sometimes the oarsmen would join in a rhythmic cry, repeating it over and over, to mark time. The cries *ō opòp ō opòp* (viz. heave ho, heave ho) and *ryppapaī* (viz. yo-ho), each one mimicking the cadence of the oar stroke, are both attested for Athenian oar crews (Ar. *Ran.* 208, 1073, *Vesp.* 909, *Av.* 1395). The learned and subversive Roman poet Ovid also speaks of how the 'rhythmic chants give time and measure to beating oars' (*Met.* 3.618–19).

Though the trireme's primary propulsion came from the 170 oars, the vessel also had two masts, a main (Gk. *histos megas*) amidships and a small foremast (Gk. *histos akateios*), with square sails, while steering was provided by two steering oars at the stern, one at the port side, one to the starboard. Sails came in two grades of linen, heavy and light. That can be explained as follows: when the wind is strong, a heavy sail is needed to prevent it from tearing. Under conditions of a light wind, a breeze, a thin sail can be made to billow by the wind, thus providing propulsion, whereas a heavy sail cannot. The naval inventories (*IG* 2² 1627.65, 1629.371, 1631.415–17) show that Athenian triremes had two suits of sails, one of which was light.

The *kubernētēs* was the highest-ranking professional seaman on a trireme, given that he was in complete charge of navigation under oar and sail. He made decisions, sometimes split-second ones, which might provide the margin of victory in battle. As the wise Nestor supposedly said to his son, 'It is by skill (*mētis*) that the helmsman holds his rapid ship on its course, though torn by winds, over the wine-dark water' (*Il.* 23.316–17). It should be said that the Greek noun *mētis* means far more than just our concept of 'skill', combining as it does the qualities of skill, cunning, craft, intelligence and ingenuity rolled into one, the very virtues of the grave, grey-eyed Athena. This quality was considered to be exceedingly estimable; Odysseus, the hero doted greatly on by Athena, being the embodiment of *mētis*.

The *kubernētēs* was assisted by the *keleustēs*, whose business was to manage the oarsmen and get the best out of them (Pl. *Alk.* 1.125C). As Xenophon makes clear:

> On a trireme, when the vessel is at sea and the oarsmen must toil all day to reach port, some *keleustaí* can say and do the right thing to sharpen the men's spirits and make them work at will, while others are so unintelligent that it takes them more than twice the time to finish the same voyage. In the first case they land bathed in sweat, with mutual congratulations, *keleustēs* and oarsmen. In the other they arrive cold, hating their rowing master. (Xen. *Oikon.* 21.3)

Clearly no *keleustēs* in his right mind would deliberately alienate his oar crew. If he did, then the ensuing bitterness and ill will would be such as to destroy the morale of the entire ship's company. Obviously one of the main tasks of the *keleustēs* was to start and stop the oar crew (Eur. *Hel.* 1590, 1595–96, Ar. *Ran.* 269). Thucydides twice mentions (2.84.3, 7.70.6) the difficulty of hearing the *keleustēs* over the din of battle, and thus good communications between him and the oar crew was thus a prerequisite for the smooth operation of any trireme. In all his tasks the *keleustēs* was probably assisted by the *aulētēs*, although there is no direct evidence for this. In Euripides' play *Hypsipyle* (61–67), Orpheus is placed amidships at the front of the mast to play his lyre to keep the Argonauts in time.

The 14 armed men and the 16 deck officers and ratings were known collectively as the *hypēresía*, or auxiliary group. They are best seen as assistants to the *triērarchos*. It is interesting to note that in democratic Athens it was possible for a sailor to come up through the ranks. Aristophanes, that most Athenian of observers, talks of a *kubernētēs*

*Olympias* at dock. Instead of a rudder hinged on the sternpost, triremes used two steering-oars, one on each side of the stern. Each was attached to a tiller (*oiax*), the ends of which were close together so that the *kubernētēs* could work both at once. He, and the *triērarchos*, who sat enthroned on the quarterdeck, were both protected by the upward curving structure of the stern. (George E. Koronaios/Wikimedia Commons/ CC BY-SA 4.0)

who had worked his way up the promotion ladder: 'Before you take the helm, first ply the oar; then for'ard stand, and study weather-lore; then you may steer' (Ar. *Eq.* 542–44). Pseudo-Xenophon ([*Ath. pol.*] 1.19–20) likewise implies that the officers were originally oarsmen who had been promoted in rank, while Plato (*Leg.* 4.707a–b), no fan of democracy, speaks of the skills of the *kubernētēs*, the *pentēkontarchos*, and the oarsman in the same breath. It appears, therefore, the navy of democratic Athens was open to all available talents regardless of social status.

Finally, we must consider the *triērarchos*. In democratic Athens the state paid for the ship and its crew: equipment and repairs were paid for by a wealthy citizen as one of the liturgies (*triērarchia*, a brilliant Athenian notion, which shamed the richest citizens into spending their wealth on the *polis*, without the need for taxation). This allowed the citizen to serve, for one year, as the commander of the trireme, *triērarchos*, he had thus sponsored. The state provided the *triērarchos* with an empty hull, probably by lot (Fornara 55.24), with the 'wooden gear' – 200 oars, two steering oars, two masts, spars, poles, a pair of boarding ladders – and the supervisors of the naval yards handed out from their stores sets of 'hanging gear' – two sails, a host of cables, ropes, side screens, awnings, and a pair of anchors – all in a condition that depended on the honesty of the previous *triērarchos*. The rest was up to him.

Surprisingly, just as the *thētes* enlisted willingly for service at sea, many rich Athenians competed to outshine their peers in the number of their annual *triērarchia*, the lavish fittings of their triremes, and the speed of their oar crews.

Marble funerary stele of Demokleides son of Demetrios (Athens, National Archaeological Museum, inv. Ap 752), of unknown provenance but probably from Athens, dated to *c*.380 BC, who died at sea serving as an *epibátēs*. The pensive young man sits on the canopy deck of the trireme in which he served, gazing at the prow. He wears a short, belted *chiton*, while his hoplite shield (*aspís*) and Corinthian helmet lay behind him. The only parts of the trireme that are shown are the curved prow and the ram, the details of which were depicted in paint, but are no longer visible. Since the Athenian trireme itself was the weapon, *epibátai* were kept to a minimum on board – Demokleides being one of ten. (© Nic Fields)

# MARINES

According to Herodotos, the Chian triremes at Lade (494 BC) each carried '40 picked men, of citizen class (viz. hoplites) serving as marines' (6.15.1). The Greek term is *epibátai*, literally 'deck soldiers'. Persian triremes, again according to Herodotos (7.96.1, 7.184.2), carried, apart from an unspecified number of native marines, 30 additional fighting men who were Persians, Medes or Scythians (OP *Sakā*), the last of whom were a nomadic people of central Asia highly valued for their archery skills. These were almost certainly crowded on board to ensure the loyalty of the ship's company and for that reason they were undoubtedly carried in battle, the Ionian Revolt having demonstrated to the Persians that their non-Persian navy could become the undoing of their domination of the eastern Mediterranean.

The ten *epibátai* on an Athenian trireme had the highest status in the trireme after the *triērarchos*. They are mentioned second in the Decree of Themistokles (Fornara 55.24–25), and this is the position they occupy in the 4th-century crew-lists (*IG* 2$^2$ 1951.79–82). They join the *triērarchos* in pouring libations from gold and silver vessels at the ceremonial

Marble panel from the acropolis of Xanthos, dated c.480–470 BC. A Greek/Lykian 'hoplite' wearing a *linothōrax* and supporting an *aspis* hands over a crested Corinthian helmet to an enthroned Kybernis of Lykia (r. 520–480 BC). Kybernis is known from Herodotos to have supplied Xerxes with 50 triremes for the invasion of Greece. (Jastrow/Wikimedia Commons/Public domain)

departure of the Sicilian expedition (Thuc. 6.32.1). When the Athenian *stratēgós* Demosthenes lost some 120 of his 300 *epibátai* from 30 triremes employed as a landing force, Thucydides says they were men 'all in the prime of life … by far the best men in Athens that fell during this war' (3.98.4). As mentioned previously, the Decree of Themistokles lists *epibátai* as recruited 'from men over 20 years of age up to 30' (Fornara 55.25–26). Fighting on deck or boarding and entering an enemy vessel required some agility, especially so if decks were slippery, and it should be expected that *epibátai* were generally not only quite young but gung-ho too. Even in 480 BC, the evidence suggests that the *epibátai* were viewed as an élite force among the pool of citizen hoplites, drawn from the fittest young men of the upper three tiers of Athenian society: the *zeugĩtai*, the *hippeĩs*, and the *pentakosiomédimnoi*.

Though *epibátai* could and did go ashore to perform combat duties as a landing party, it is likely that their principal function was disciplinary. In other words, this was to reinforce the authority of the *triērarchos*, for Aristotle speaks of them as having 'the command and control' (*Pol.* 1327b8) aboard ship. In addition to furnishing their *triērarchos* with latent support, another good reason for the Athenian practice of taking only a few hoplites on deck to serve as *epibátai* was due to pulling efficiency. This was seriously jeopardized if there were many moving about topside and inevitably caused the ship to roll and so spoil the oarsmen's stroke. Under oar, therefore, the *epibátai* had to be seated (Thuc. 7.67.2), and the procedure appears to have been to keep them centred on the middle line of the ship. When it had come to a stop locked onto an enemy vessel and expecting boarders, the *epibátai* would of course have done no harm

# SEAPOWER, STRATEGY AND SUPPLY

The success of any maritime empire built on oared warships depended on its control of strategically situated coastal sites that offered potable water – each oarsman needed 7.6 litres of drinking water per day to stay hydrated – fresh provisions – the wineskins containing coarse wine (what the French would call *piquette*), cloves of garlic, olives, nets of onions, and anchovies of the oarsmen featured in Aristophanes (*Eq.* 550–1, 600) – and protection from foul weather. A trireme had to put to shore twice a day so as to feed and rest the crew.

Triremes were ill-suited to blockading coastal towns or cities, or even islands. The only effective approach was to station naval detachments along key routes in such a manner that any one of them was in a position to monitor any enemy shipping either approaching or leaving the objective, and so, with any luck, intercept the target.

Seapower in our period of study had its distinct limitations, and the trireme was essentially designed for battle.

Nevertheless, Athens could reach as far as Cyprus, Egypt or southern Italy, locations 1,000km from Peiraieus. Much closer to home, Athens could raid up and down the Peloponnesian coast, bringing ruin and spreading terror. Tolmides did exactly this with a fleet of 50 triremes in 456 BC, coasting along from one target to the next, burning the Spartan naval yards, capturing the Corinthian *polis* of Chalkis and, 'after making a landing at Sikyon, defeated the Sikyonians in battle' (Thuc. 1.108.3). However, unless admirals were prepared to risk their hoplites ashore, as Tolmides evidently was during his amphibious campaign, they were limited as to what they could achieve. Plato grumbled that the hoplites involved in naval raids, instead of feeling duty bound to stand their ground as they would in the hoplite phalanx, 'are in the habit of constantly leaping down from their ships and then quickly retreating to their vessels at a run, and see nothing shameful in this' (*Leg.* 4.706c).

# ATHENIAN FIGHTING COMPLEMENT

(A) *Epibatēs* (Greek citizen hoplite)
1. *aspís* (bronze-faced shield)
2. *linothōrax* (stiff linen corselet)
3. *knēmides* (bronze greaves)
4. Corinthian-style helmet ('at ease' position)
5. *pteruges* (strips, for ease of movement)
6. *dóru* (long-thrusting spear)
7. *kópis* (heavy, single-edged sword)

(B) Scythian *toxotēs* (mercenary archer)
8. loose-fitting tunic
9. soft leather cap
10. composite recurve bow
11. *akīnákes* (double-edged sword)
12. *gorytós* (bow case and quiver)
13. *ságarìs* (iron battleaxe)

by standing up and moving. So, they would leap up to fight once ships grappled. The Athenian *stratēgós* Nikias, in his speech exhorting the doomed men at Syracuse before the final sea battle in the Great Harbour, reveals another reason. He says:

> Many archers and javelineers will be on deck and a mass of hoplites, which we would not employ if we were fighting a battle in the open sea, because they would hinder us through the weight of the ships in exercising our skill. (Thuc. 7.62.2)

The Lenormant relief with its associated fragment, giving the midship section of the starboard side of an Athenian trireme under oar, depicts a canopy deck on which men are lying. Weight, particularly on deck, prevented Athenian triremes doing what they did best, namely bringing off the breakthrough, the *diékplous*, and the circling movement, the *períplous*, tactical manoeuvres in which speed and agility were essential.

# ARCHERS

Aischylos (*Pérs.* 454–61, cf. Plut. *Them.* 14.1) notes how *toxótai* fought alongside *epibátai* at Salamis. On the other hand, in the Decree of Themistokles (Fornara 55.26), the four *toxótai* assigned to each trireme are clearly distinct from the ten *epibátai*, that is to say, they are not carried on the canopy deck. An inscription (*IG* 1² 950.137), dated to 412/411 BC, gives them a descriptive adjective *páredroi* – sitting beside. It seems that they were posted in the stern beside the *triērarchos* and *kubernētēs* on the quarterdeck and acted as their bodyguard in action. The latter would certainly have been vulnerable and would have needed protection, being too busy steering the vessel to defend himself. The Athenian playwright Euripides (*IT* 1377), who wrote in the heyday of trireme use, writes of archers stationed in the stern providing covering fire during an embarkation.

According to Aischines, sometime after Xerxes' invasion of Greece, the Athenians 'fortified Peiraieus … equipped 300 horsemen and bought 300 Scythians' (2.173); Thucydides says it was Themistokles who 'persuaded them [the Athenians] to finish the walls of Peiraieus, which had been begun before, in his year of office as *árchōn*' (1.93.3, cf. Plut. *Them.* 19.2). In his *On the Peace*, which dates from 392/391 BC, Andokides reports the same incident (though he gets the date wrong), but specifies that these Scythians were archers: 'It was at this time that we first enrolled 300 horsemen and purchased 300 Scythian archers' (3.5).

The Scythians were 'other', alien and therefore a little unnerving. Even so, by this time the Scythian archer had already become a familiar character in the streets of Athens, where he was exploited, and sometimes ridiculed (as a savage, stammering,

Black-figure tondo from Attic bilingual *kylix* (Paris, Musée du Louvre, inv. F 126), wine cup, by the Oltos Painter, dated to 530–520 BC. This shows a Scythian archer drawing an arrow from his *gorytos*. (Tilemachos Efthimiadis/Wikimedia Commons/CC BY-SA 2.0)

drunken barbarian), by the populace (Ar. *Lys.* 184, *Thesm.* 1002, Anakreon 76 apud Ath. 11.427a). The Scythian was probably the most common Oriental 'type' encountered in 5th-century BC Athens, as Scythian archers (*toxótai*, literally '[the] archers') served as an urban police force (Ar. *Ach.* 54, 707, *Ekkl.* 143, 258–9, *Eq.* 665, *Lys.* 445, 451, *Thesm.* 923).

The composite recurve bow, the Scythian weapon *par excellence*, was also the Persian weapon of choice. Somewhat long by contemporary standards (*c.*1.2m), Xenophon (*Anab.* 3.3.7, 3.3.15, 3.4.17) himself was witness to the fact that the Persian bow could easily outrange that used by the Cretans, the most famous specialist archers of antiquity, though the Cretans could perform long-range shooting at a high trajectory with captured Persian arrows. This suggests that the greater Persian range was the result of lighter arrows and different training, rather than any difference in bow technology. Cretan archers used large, heavy arrowheads with barbs, whereas Persian heads were usually three-edged, some 3–4cm long and socketed. The socketed heads were fitted to a wooden fore shaft, which was in turn inserted into the main shaft, light, hollow, and made from reed. With their triangular sectioned bronze or iron tips, these relatively lightweight arrows were more effective against un-armoured targets than for penetrating shield or body armour.

All the same, as a symbol of kingship and the Persian national arm, the bow was held in the hand of the Great King in his sculptures and on his coins. Hence Xerxes boasted, 'I will conquer Greece with my archers'. This was something of a pun – intentional or otherwise – as the gold Daric (Gk. *dareikós*) was popularly known by the Greeks as the 'archer' (Plut. *Artax.* 20.4, *Ages.* 15.6). The obverse of this golden coin bore the device of a crowned 'running archer', a bearded man dressed in the Persian calf-length tunic with long sleeves, holding his bow and arrow ready to shoot with one knee bent as if in motion – the Great King himself, armed with arrows and ready to take down victims at a distance.

The 'drawn bow' stands in Aischylos' *Pérsai* as a symbol for Persia to the degree that the 'bronze-head spear' does for Greece (145–46). At the start of the tragedy the grandees of Persia, stern and dignified and setting forth for Greece, are called 'masters of bow and bridle' (*Pérs.* 26), while at its end the young king, Xerxes himself, ill-tempered and ineffective and back home in Sousa, has lost his bow and his quiver is empty (*Pérs.* 1018–23).

We must remember that the bow was not a typical Greek weapon. The Greeks themselves used a self-bow made of a single flexible wooden staff, with seasoned woods, such as elm and yew, providing far greater properties of compression and release. Power was improved by cutting the bow staff so that the sapwood sat on the face of the bow, while the heartwood was on the inside. The sapwood was more flexible, meaning the bow could be drawn back further, while the heartwood gave good properties of compression. On the other hand, Cretan archers, often serving as mercenaries throughout the Mediterranean world, used a composite recurve bow, as did Scythian archers, who, if not in Persian service, were also employed at this time by Greek *poleis*, especially Athens.

Attic red-figure *pinax* (London, British Museum, inv. GR 1837 0609.59) signed by the painter Epikteto, from the Etruscan necropolis at Vulci and dated to 520–510 BC. Scythian archers appear on a number of Athenian vases, always gaily clothed in patterned sleeved tunics and baggy trousers in bright contrasting colours and decorated with stitching and embroidery work, and soft leather caps. The clothing was well designed for steppe life, comfortable, warm and windproof. Ovid was familiar with Scythians from the time of his miserable exile in remote Tomis (Constanţa, Romania), where showers of poisonous arrows could come whizzing over the walls at any moment, or so he claims. He says of them: 'With stitched breeches (*bracis*) and sewn skins covering all but face, the savage grapples with grim winter' (*Tr.* 3.10.19–20). On Athenian vases they are more often than not associated with the composite recurve bow and *gorytós*, and the copious iconography on objects recovered from the elite burials on the Pontic steppe is a reminder that the Scythian was seldom parted from his bow, even in repose. (ArchaiOptix/Wikimedia Commons/CC BY-SA 4.0)

Detail of fresco depicting a Lykian warrior, painted tomb chamber at Kızıbel near Emalı, central Lykia, dated c.525 BC. Despite Lykia falling under Persian domination after 546 BC, it enjoyed considerable autonomy, a situation reflected in sculptural art, which was Greek in style and Lykian in expression. The skeletal remains suggest that the deceased was a well-built, active male in his fifties, a warrior. (Wikimedia Commons/Public Domain)

This may in part explain why the full value of archers was only gradually appreciated in Greece towards the end of the Peloponnesian War, which had lasted for over a quarter of a century and set the entire Hellenic world at odds. There is some suggestion in Greek literature that archers were generally despised. It was Euripides, for instance, who said the test of man's courage was not the bow, a coward's weapon, but 'to stand and look and outface the spear's swift stroke, keeping the line firm' (*HF* 162–64).

Certainly 'spindles' (Gk. *átraktoi*, i.e. arrows) were regarded by the Spartans as the weapons of the womanly and weak (Thuc. 4.40.2), in contrast to the spear and shield of the face-to-face, toe-to-toe hoplite warrior. The austere Spartans prided themselves on their martial virtue; one Spartan at Thermopylai (of hallowed memory) is reported to have quipped that he did not mind if the Persians' arrow storm was so thick that it blocked out the sun, since he preferred to do his fighting in the shade (Hdt. 7.226.1).

A. Phoenician marine
1. Greek-style helmet
2. *thōrēkas linéous*
   (linen corselet)
3. Greek-style shield
4. *pteruges* (strips, for
   ease of movement)
5. *drépanon* (single-edged
   sickle-sword)
6. *dórata te naúmacha*
   ('boarding-spear')
7. javelins
Note: the above terms are
Greek ones, as given by
Herodotos (7.89.1, 3).

# COMBAT

## NAVAL TACTICS

There were two main methods of fighting, which placed contradictory demands on trireme design. The first was ramming. This called for the smallest possible ship built around the largest number of rowers. The Athenian navy with its small number of onboard marines followed this philosophy with regards to naval architecture. The other was entering and boarding. This called for larger, heavier ships able to carry the maximum number of marines, with the end result of a slower and less manoeuvrable ship. The Chians at Lade, for example, with their 40 marines per trireme, followed this robust philosophy. The latter view eventually prevailed, since, to ram, a vessel had to make contact, which was just what the boarders wanted. Hence the later development of larger vessels with complete, broad decks (Athenian triremes were only partially decked), namely the four-, five- and six-banked ships of the Hellenistic period, which were primarily designed as heavily armoured floating platforms to carry towers, ballistae and marines, and so lent themselves to none of the naval tactics on which the Athenian triremes had relied.

The manoeuvre-and-ram school, in which the Athenian navy was to reign supreme, relied on two main manoeuvres, the *diékplous* and the *períplous*, which are summarized in the illustration opposite. Still, there were two countermoves to the *diékplous* and *períplous*: first, to occupy a position that was enclosed enough so as to restrict the full use of the *diékplous* (Thuc. 7.36); or, if in open water, form a defensive circle (*kúklos*) with rams pointing outward towards the enemy (Thuc. 2.83.5, 3.78.1). The alternative, especially for a large fleet, was to form up in double line abeam (Xen. *Hell.* 1.6.28), making the *diékplous* suicidal. The disadvantage, of course, was that it shortened the battleline, leaving a fleet vulnerable to the *períplous*.

# TACTICAL MANOEUVRES

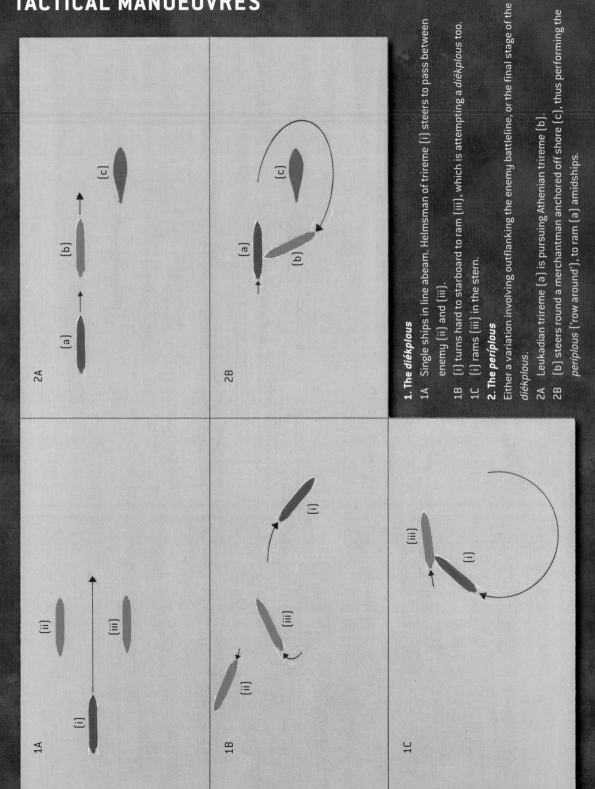

**1. The *diékplous***

1A   Single ships in line abeam. Helmsman of trireme (i) steers to pass between enemy (ii) and (iii).

1B   (i) turns hard to starboard to ram (iii), which is attempting a *diékplous* too.

1C   (i) rams (iii) in the stern.

**2. The *períplous***

Either a variation involving outflanking the enemy battleline, or the final stage of the *diékplous*.

2A   Leukadian trireme (a) is pursuing Athenian trireme (b).

2B   (b) steers round a merchantman anchored off shore (c), thus performing the *períplous* ('row around'), to ram (a) amidships.

# LADE (494 BC)

At the naval battle of Lade, an island off the coast of Miletos, the Ionian Greeks and their island allies assembled 353 triremes: 80 from Miletos, 12 from Priene, three from Myous, 17 from Teos, eight from Erythrai, and three from Phokaia, while the three great eastern Aegean islands of Chios, Samos and Lesbos provided 100, 60 and 70 respectively. Nonetheless, this was only a little more than half the size of the Persian naval force of 600 triremes, the largest, and best crewed, contingent coming from Phoenicia. The commander was probably Dātis the Mede, famous for his command at Marathon four years later, with among his subordinates the nephew of Dareios I, Mardonios.

Herodotos (6.9.1) notes that the Persian strategy was to carry out an amphibious operation against Miletos, attacking with an army and sending a fleet with contingents from Phoenicia, Cyprus, Cilicia and Egypt. The Persians were not expecting a naval battle but hoping to force Miletos to surrender with a land and naval blockade. Since the Persians were accustomed to using their navy as a transport and means of blockade they were, upon arriving off Lade, surprised and diffident upon seeing a foe prepared to fight a sea battle.

The Phokaian naval tactician Dionysios was put in charge of the Ionian fleet. Normally the position of command was accorded to an officer whose *polis* supplied the largest contingent (in this case Chios), but Phokaia had only provided one of the smallest contingents – the Phokaians had chosen to emigrate with their families and possessions rather than accept Persian rule (they had founded Massilia, modern Marseille, around 600 BC); though some became homesick and returned (Hdt. 1.163–67), hence the reduced size of their state. According to Herodotos (6.11–12) Dionysios promised to teach them in a short time naval tactics which would either discourage the Persian fleet from going to battle or bring about a Persian defeat.

For seven days Dionysios took them to sea in a line-ahead formation instructing the oarsmen how 'to carry out the manoeuvre known as the breakthrough' (Hdt. 6.12.1), that is to say, the *diékplous*, and kept the marines on the decks under arms. Eventually, the Ionians balked at this exhausting manoeuvre which required long days of strenuous physical training to develop strength, endurance, skill and teamwork of a high order among the oar crews. These were the qualities needed to produce a burst of speed to deliver a precise blow on the beam of the opposing ship – it is clear at a later date that Athenian supremacy at sea was largely the result of constant training (Thuc. 1.142.6–9). After seven days, 'worn out with hardship and the sun' (Hdt. 6.12.2), the oarsmen and the marines stopped practising, claiming that it was a form of slavery, and retired to their tents ('We have lost our minds and launched out into folly, committing ourselves into the hands of this Phokaian braggart, who brings but three ships' [Hdt. 6.12.3]).

Proceeding line ahead, the Ionians commenced the battle: Herodotos (6.8.1–2) gives the order of the Ionian battle line as being, from east to west, Miletos–Priene–Myous–Teos–Chios–Erythrai–Phokaia–Lesbos–Samos. Demoralized by the breakdown in training the Samians, save 11 steadfast triremes, deserted the cause and fled for their island home, and they were followed by the Lesbian contingent and other deserters. Without striking a blow, the whole west wing of the Ionian battle line quickly collapsed and took to flight. Herodotos notes that the Samians hoisted their sails and sailed away. Triremes, generally, did not go into battle with sails; these were normally stowed away, the mainsails together with any other gear unnecessary for immediate purpose being left ashore before battle (Thuc. 7.24.2, Xen. *Hell.* 6.2.27). Clearing for action was an essential pre-battle task, for even when lowered, the spars and ropes made for a cluttered deck, which would have badly impeded the marines. The Samian contingent, which held the left wing on the west of the Greek battleline, may have insisted on taking the sails aboard to aid them to escape to nearby Samos in case of certain defeat. The Chians, however, stationed in the centre, had no escape route nor did they wish it, and with 100 ships and the few remaining Ionians, apparently used the *diékplous* successfully but were eventually overwhelmed by the greater number of Persian triremes (Hdt. 6.15.2). However, there is reason to suspect the use of this manoeuvre by the Chians, for their strong contingent of 40 marines (Hdt. 6.15.1) is indicative of a different tactical concept, namely boarding and entering.

While we are on the topic of the *diékplous*, at about the time of Themistokles' birth, in a naval battle off Alalia (Aléria, Corsica), 60 Phokaian warships (probably *pentēkónteroi*, cf. Hdt. 1.163.2) defeated a Punic-Etruscan fleet twice their own size. This was no miracle. The Phokaians had apparently relied on the rams they had affixed to their ships and the skill of their helmsmen rather than a head-on boarding action. But the price of victory did not come cheap, 'for 40 of their vessels were destroyed and the remaining 20 had their rams (*émboloi*) so badly bent as to render them unfit for service' (Hdt. 1.166.2). It looks as if the weapon was still in the early stages of development and, correspondingly, the art of ramming was still in a rudimentary stage. Nevertheless, this naval battle was the prelude to enormous changes in the tactics of naval warfare, foreshadowing as it did the age of the trireme in the following century when the ships themselves began to be used as weapons.

The Phokaians, having acquired naval skills in their nautical struggles against the Carthaginians and Etruscans in the western Mediterranean, were ideally placed to teach their fellow Ionians the *diékplous* before Lade. However, the Ionian leadership could not control the great number of men so recently pressed into naval service, let alone force them to submit to the arduous training in rowing and seamanship that might have granted them victory at Lade. When triremes served as transports, ambassadorial ships, anti-pirate craft, there was less need for the firm discipline and steadfast solidarity required in successfully performing difficult manoeuvres such as the *diékplous*.

Miletos was besieged by land and sea, and razed to the ground: a layer of ash and debris, several metres deep in places, has been found between the classical and archaic levels throughout the city. Its surviving inhabitants were enslaved or deported; some Milesians were forced to settle in Ampe, near the mouth of the Tigris (Hdt. 6.20).

Büyük Menderes (ancient Maeander) river panorama looking north from the North Agora, Miletos (Milet). Now the sea is far away, thanks to the unceasing labour of the Maeander, fittingly called 'the worker' by Herodotos (cf. Strab. 15.1.16). The small island of Lade (Batiköy), north-west of the ruins of Miletos, has long since been united to the mainland by the silt of the Maeander. What remains today is a chain of three inconspicuous hills on the flood plain of the Büyük Menderes, two of which can be seen in the far left middle distance. On the right is the tip of former peninsula of Miletos and in the far distance Samsun Dağı (elev. 1,237m), ancient Mount Mykale and site of a Persian defeat in 479 BC. (Tomisti/Wikimedia Commons/ CC BY-SA 4.0)

# BRIDGES OF BOATS

Xerxes, unlike the foolish and headstrong autocrat as portrayed in Herodotos, was meticulous in his strategic planning for the invasion of mainland Greece (480–479 BC). Three years were spent cutting a canal through the isthmus of the Mount Athos peninsula so that his fleet would not have to chance the dangers of rounding the stormy promontory (Hdt. 7.22–23). What is more, the first pontoon bridges which we undoubtedly recall from history – even if 30 years earlier his father Dareios I, also known as 'the Great', had bridged 'the Bosporus that teems with fish' (Hdt. 4.85–88) – were the two built by Xerxes across the 'broad Hellespont' – today's Dardanelles, a slender strip of salt sea separating the two continents of Asia and Europe.

Built near its south-western end nearby Abydos, the narrowest point of the Hellespont, the pontoon bridges, stretching to Sestos, were seven *stadia* (*c*.1,344m) in length when completed and ready for use. As usual, the Fates had other ideas. A violent storm broke them whereupon the Great King got even by throwing two pairs of shackles into the sea, and ordering his men to give it 300 strokes of a whip and to brand it with red-hot irons, while he addressed it in imperious language. Then he ordered all those persons who had been charged with the construction of the bridges to be beheaded (Hdt. 7.34–35).

Immediately afterwards he had two new pontoon bridges constructed, which lay side by side. There were 360 *pentēkóntoroi* and triremes positioned under the first bridge, and 314 under the second. Great cables, of flax and papyrus, were used to lash the ships together, while anchors fixed them in place. Wooden planks were then laid across the cables, with brushwood and earth to cover the planks and form a natural roadway, which allowed Xerxes' army to walk into Europe. The crossing took seven days and nights (Hdt. 7.36, 7.56.1). All Greece held its breath.

As the eventual inheritors of the Assyrians, this was an action by the Persians consistent with a long-standing Near Eastern policy of resettlement. In Athens the news of these events was received with alarm. Shortly after the Athenian tragedian Phrynichos (*fl.* 511–476 BC) staged a play (now completely lost) called the *Fall of Miletos*, and the audience was moved to tears; Phrynichos was fined 1,000 Attic drachmae 'for bringing to mind a calamity that affected them so personally' (Hdt. 6.21.2, cf. Strab. 14.1.7), Miletos having 'been founded by Athenian settlers' (Hdt. 5.97.2). As a result, the play was banned from being performed again.

As for Dionysios the Phokaian, he made good his escape. Having taken three enemy vessels in the battle, he sailed not to Phokaia, knowing well that there was not refuge there, but 'right away sailed to Phoenicia instead, sunk some merchant ships, took a lot of money, and sailed to Sicily; from this base he set himself up as a pirate, robbing Carthaginians and Tyrrhenians [Etruscans], but no Greeks' (Hdt. 6.17). Even though he only commanded three triremes, the buccaneering career of Dionysios caused the Phoenicians, Carthaginians, and Etruscans a lot of damage, preying on their wealth to maintain himself and his comrades.

# ARTEMISION (480 BC)

Herodotos gives the size of the Persian fleet as 1,207 triremes (7.89–95, 7.184.1) with an addition of 120 ships from the Greeks of Thrace and its offshore islands (7.185.1). It seems possible that he is recording here the paper strength of the Persian navy and not the operation number of Xerxes' invasion fleet, though it is interesting to note that Aischylos (*Pérs.* 341–43), who witnessed the battle, gives the same original figure albeit for the battle of Salamis. This figure has often been questioned (and notoriously emended to a more modest one) but it does not have to be. The figures for Xerxes' army and his navy are disparate, having been arrived at in very different ways. As John Lazenby points out, 'it is worth remembering that ships are much easier to count than men' (1993: 94).

Artemision took its name from a small shore side temple erected there dedicated to the goddess Artemis 'Facing the East' (*Prosēōia*), this epithet arising from the fact that it was here that ships took their departure eastwards across the Aegean. The temple itself overlooked a long curving beach on the northern coast of Euboia. The Persian fleet, now reduced by storm losses, was beached at a string of little beaches known as Aphetai ('Starting Places') just opposite Artemision some 16km to the north-east.

On realization that the Greeks were nearby the Persians detached a force of 200 triremes and despatched them southwards on a route along the seaward coast of Euboia to round the island and cut the enemy's line of retreat via the long winding strait that separates Euboia from the mainland (Hdt. 8.8.3). Their intention was to offer battle as soon as they heard that this was cut. The Greeks, on the other hand, 'desiring to put to the proof his fashion of fighting and the art of breaking the line' (Hdt 8.9), came out late in that first day so that the action should not last long. The customary hour for a naval engagement was early morning, the time of calm winds and flat waters; the Greeks appreciated that in a protracted engagement the overriding numbers of the Persian fleet would eventually tell. In response the Persian crews, who could hardly believe their eyes, quickly manned their ships confidently expecting an easy victory 'since they saw the Greek ships were few while their own were many times more numerous and better sailing' (Hdt. 8.10.1), and encircled the Greek ships.

This was the naval tactic known as the *diékplous*, literally 'a rowing through and out'. In this hazardous manoeuvre, a single trireme or, preferably, triremes in single

The Greek anchorage prior to the three-day naval engagement off Artemision has been identified as the broad, open beach at Pévki bay, 10km west of Cape Artemision. West of Pévki the sheltered sandy beaches stretch out in an almost unbroken chain along the north coast of Euboia (Evvía), and the Greek triremes would have ample space to beach in a single line. A Roman period inscription unearthed in 1883 at what was once the temple of Artemis Prosēōia (now occupied by the chapel of Áyios Yeóryios) confirmed the identification of Cape Artemision. The inscription details contributions for repairs to the sanctuary. The shore side temple is mentioned by Herodotos ('a temple of Artemis', 7.176.1) and Plutarch ('a small temple of Artemis, named Prosēōia', *Them.* 8.2) in their respective accounts of the naval battle. (© Nic Fields)

line abreast, rowed through a gap in the enemy line, quickly came about to ram in side or stern. In response the Greeks changed formation from single line abreast facing the enemy, in which they could have been outflanked in open water, and 'formed into a close circle, with bows outward and sterns to the centre' (Hdt. 8.11.1). The Greeks succeeded in taking 30 vessels, and nightfall put an end to the battle before the Persians could turn the tide.

Normally this defensive tactic was only employed by a slower, weaker fleet, but it is hard to imagine 271 triremes, the nominal strength of the Greek fleet on this day, forming a circle, which would have measured some 5km in circumference, and one wonders if triremes were capable of remaining in station in such a formation (cf. Thuc. 2.83–84). Yet, unlike Thucydides (2.83.5), Herodotos does not actually use the term 'circle' (*kúklos*) in his narrative, but as already noted, he employs the phraseology 'with bows outward and sterns to the centre', in other words the Greek line was bent like bow, curved back in an immense convex arc. So, the Greeks compelled the enemy to ram prow to prow, and, in the end, brought about a mêlée in which speed and manoeuvrability of the enemy triremes was of little or no advantage.

The following night a second summer storm, accompanied by torrential rain, drove the 200-ship force upon the rocks of Euboia's windswept and treacherous eastern coast, off what Herodotos calls 'the Hollows of Euboia' (8.13), and all were wrecked. The Hollows had a bad name among Greek sailors (Eur. *Tro.* 84), but as the Delphic oracle had predicted, the winds seemed to be fighting for the Greeks. Next morning – likewise the second day of fighting at Thermopylai – news of the destruction of the Persian task force reached the Greek fleet, and shortly afterwards further Athenian reinforcements of 53 triremes arrived. Herodotos says almost nothing about the second day's fighting off Artemision. The Greeks again came out late in the day against some Cilician ships and 'having destroyed them, when night came, they sailed back to Artemision' (Hdt. 8.14.2).

Finally, on the third day, the frustrated Persian admirals, thinking of Xerxes' anger at those who failed him, put to sea first, arranging their ships in a sickle-shaped formation as the fleet rowed out from the coast of Magnesia. At first the Greeks made no move, but as the enemy approached the beach at Artemision, they came out in full force, and took the initiative in attack. The Persian ships apparently fell back in some confusion, but did not break their line, and the two fleets separated after some bitter fighting and heavy casualties on both sides. The most formidable fighters that day had been the heavily armed Egyptian marines. In Herodotos' catalogue of Xerxes' invasion armada they are described as wearing 'reticulated helmets and were armed with concave, broad-rimmed shields, boarding-spears, and heavy battleaxes, and most of them also wore corselets and carried long knives' (7.89.2). Appropriate arms for close-quarter action aboard ship, and by the end of the day they had carried five Greek triremes by boarding and taking them 'together with their crews' (Hdt. 8.17).

That evening the Greeks heard the fate of Leonidas at Thermopylai and took the decision to withdraw southwards that very night, abandoning Euboia (and Attica) to the enemy. The contemporary Theban poet, Pindar, may have been right when he said that Artemision was the 'great fight where the brave sons of Athens planted the shining cornerstone of their freedom' (apud Plut. *Them.* 8.2), yet it was to be the heroic last stand at Thermopylai that soon began to act as an inspiration to the Greeks.

Aerial view of Salamis Strait looking north, with Ákra Kinósoura (formerly Varvári) in the foreground. Jutting into the sea eastwards towards Peiraieus, this narrow, hilly tongue of land is ancient Kynósoura – 'dog's tail' (cf. Plut. *Them.* 10.6). Offering shelter from both the southerly winds and the waves of the Saronic Gulf, Kynósoura protected the harbour, today known as Órmos Ambelakíon, of the ancient town of Salamis (Kamateró). Opposite on the Attic mainland is the Peiraieus suburb of Pérama with Mount Aigaleos behind. 'Pounded by the sea', as Sophokles (*Aj.* 598) described Salamis, but the waters of this island are no longer pellucid but polluted. They are also choked by rusting shipping, laid up and awaiting the breakers' yard. (Jona Lendering/Wikimedia Commons/CC0 1.0)

# SALAMIS (480 BC)

The Greek admirals' plans were apparently varied – among them was Themistokles' hope to stay and fight it out in the home waters of Salamis Strait. Apparently, Themistokles had interpreted the second Delphic oracle (to his favour) prior to Artemision. Oracles were never clear at the best of times, but like most powerful people, he found ways either to ignore or to exploit unpleasant oracles. On this particular occasion Themistokles chose the latter option.

One verse of the second oracle contains the enigmatic phrase 'the wooden wall' as well as the reference to Salamis. Naturally there was considerable debate amongst the Athenians about its meaning. Some of the older men maintained that by 'the wooden wall' Apollo had meant the Acropolis, which had been fenced about with a wooden palisade. However, those who argued that 'ships' was the meaning were worried by the reference to Salamis, since those skilled in the interpretation of oracles took this to mean that they would be defeated off Salamis. At this critical point, Themistokles came forward and settled the issue:

> If, he maintained, the disaster referred to was to strike the Athenians, it would not have been expressed in such mild language. 'Hateful Salamis' would surely have been a more likely phrase than 'divine Salamis', if the inhabitants of the country were doomed to destruction there … so he advised his countrymen to prepare at once to meet the invader at sea … And they determined in debate after the discussion on the oracle, to take the god's advice and meet the invader at sea with all the force they possessed, and with any other Greeks who were willing to join them. (Hdt. 7.144)

So Themistokles interpreted the 'wooden wall' as the Hellenic League fleet, and argued that Salamis would bring death to the Persians, not the Greeks.

No such frustrations for Xerxes, for his intentions were clear: the Great King wanted to destroy the Hellenic League fleet before completing his conquest of Greece

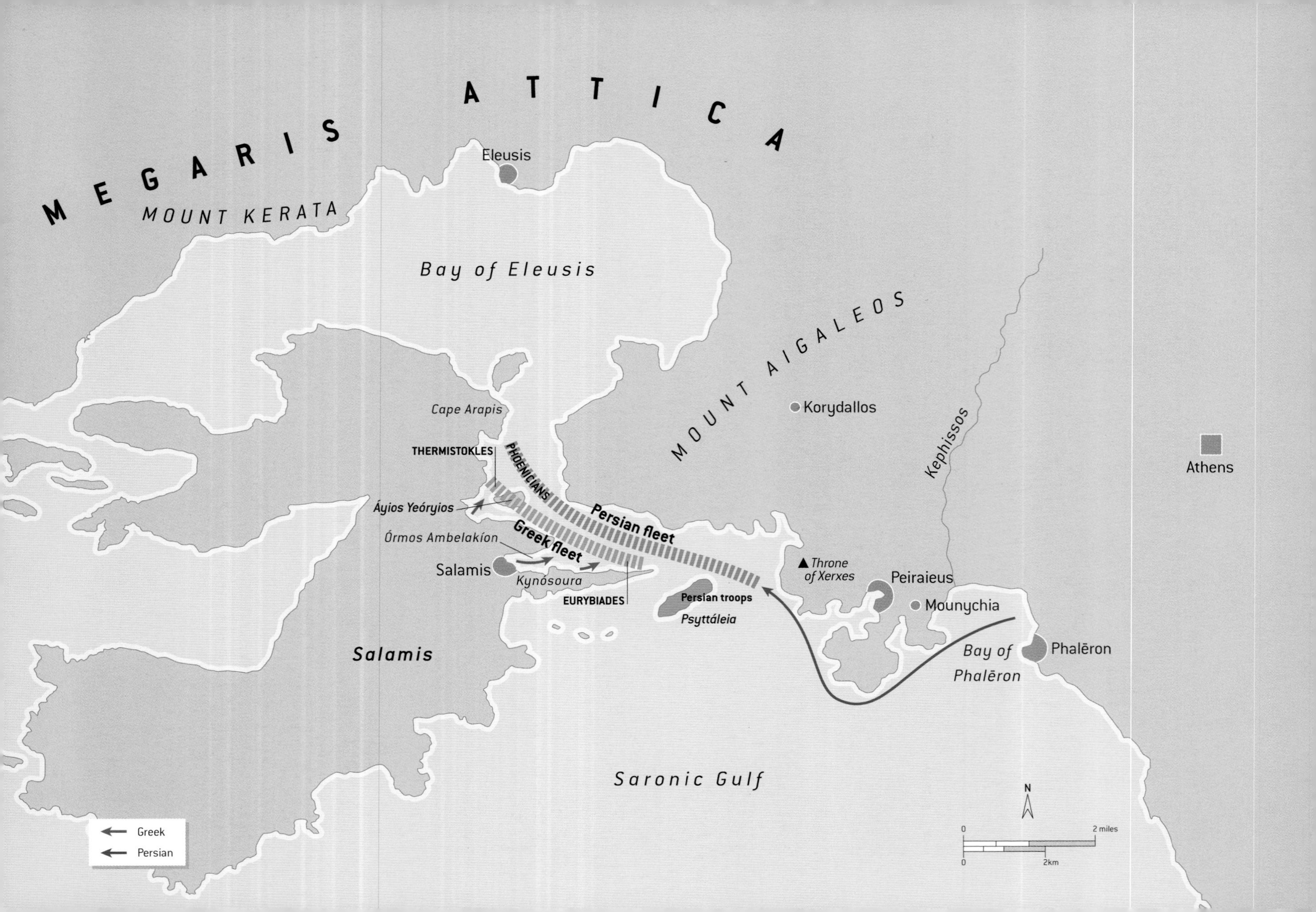

Athens

Phalēron

Bay of
Phalēron

Mounychia

*Kephissos*

Peiraieus

Korydallos

A T T I C A

M O U N T   A I G A L E O S

▲ *Throne
of Xerxes*

Persian troops

*Psyttáleia*

Saronic Gulf

Persian fleet

PHOENICIANS

Greek fleet

EURYBIADES

*Kynósoura*

Eleusis

Bay of Eleusis

Cape Arapis

THERMISTOKLES

*Áyios Yeóryios*

*Órmos Ambelákion*

Salamis

Salamis

M E G A R I S

MOUNT KERATA

N

2 miles

2km

0

0

Greek

Persian

by invading the Peloponnese. In the meantime, Attica had been abandoned (Hdt. 8.41) and the Hellenic League fleet, which had held its own only to retreat from Artemision on hearing the fate of Leonidas, took station off the rugged island of Salamis, the legendary home of the hero Ajax. It was here, in the strip of sea between the modern town of Ambelákia on Salamis and the suburb of Pérama on the Attic coast, that the final reckoning with Xerxes' navy took place.

It is possible that the Persian fleet was induced to move into the fatal sheet of water between Salamis and the Attic mainland during the night by a message from Themistokles. Aischylos' version (*Pérs.* 357–60) of the message is simple and straightforward: as soon as night had fallen, the Greeks would no longer stay in their position but would flee furtively in all directions, plainly a matter of a rash *sauve qui peut* reaction. Herodotos says the same more pithily – 'the Greeks are afraid and are planning to slip away' (8.75.2) – but has an important addition, the disclosure that the Greeks were no longer united and their fragile alliance was on the brink of collapse, that pro- and anti-Persian factions would even come to blows. In this version it is emphasized Themistokles is the sender and that he is pro-Persian. Thucydides (1.74.1) certainly believed in the story of the message. He has an Athenian envoy at Sparta claim that Themistokles was mainly responsible for the engagement taking place in the Salamis Strait. He also quotes from Themistokles' letter to Artaxerxes in which the Athenian refers to his 'forewarning from Salamis of the retreat' (1.137.4). Whether or not we choose to treat the message episode with scepticism, the Greeks were informed of the Persian nocturnal movements by a deserter and were ready and waiting for them just as the light was starting to leak into the sky and faint outlines were becoming visible.

It is unclear exactly what happened, and even the numbers are uncertain, though the Greeks appear to have had 300 to 400 triremes – Aischylos says the Greek numbers 'amounted to ten times thirty, and … a chosen [*ékkritos*, literary 'outstanding'] squadron of ten' (*Pérs.* 339–40); Thucydides (1.74.1) reports a claim the Greeks had 400 triremes, a slight exaggeration; Herodotos says that the Greeks had 378 triremes and adds that two triremes defected to the Greeks from the Persians, bringing the total up to 380 (Hdt. 8.48, 8.82.2), whereas when he cites the trireme numbers *polis* by *polis*, the figures add up only to 366 triremes (Hdt. 8.43–48), making the total 368 if we add the two defectors. Of the total, 180 were triremes belonging to Athens:

> These 180 ships were manned by the Athenians only, for the Plataians did not serve with them at the battle of Salamis, because during the withdrawal from Artemision, when the fleet was off Chalkis, they landed in Boiotia on the opposite shore and set about conveying their property and households to a place of safety, and were consequently left behind. (Hdt. 8.44.1)

The landlubber Plataians had willingly volunteered to row a number of Athenian triremes at Artemision, 'not that they had any knowledge of seamanship, but because of mere valour and zeal' (Hdt. 8.1.1).

The Persians certainly had rather more, perhaps somewhere between 600 and 700 triremes. The original invasion armada of 1,207 triremes which Xerxes had mustered had been whittled down by huge losses in a violent north-easterly gale off the rocky coast of Magnesia, the loss of 200 triremes wrecked off Euboia, and the battle losses

**OPPOSITE**

The Battle of Salamis, 480 BC.

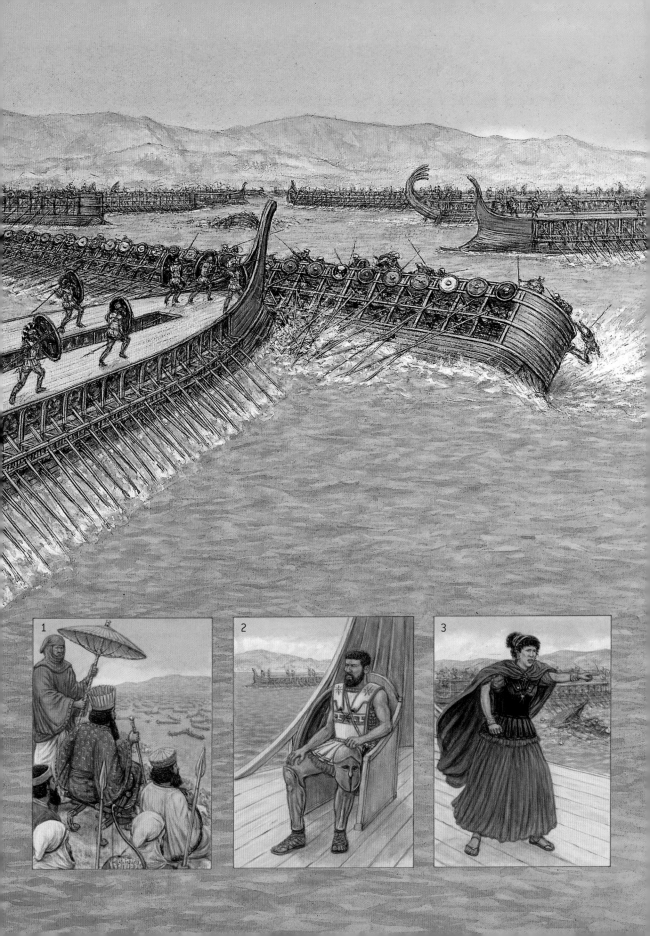

incurred during the three engagements off Artemision. However, it should be noted
that Herodotos does say (8.66.2) that these losses had been made up, and, indeed, that
120 triremes from the Greeks of Thrace and the islands of the northern Aegean had
joined the Persian fleet (7.185.1).

Herodotos, obviously one of our chief sources (the other is Aischylos' *Pérsai*),
implies it was a crowded and confused battle, but some incidents he does record. One
trireme from Samothraki, a Greek island in the northern Aegean, fighting for the
Persians, rammed and disabled an Athenian trireme, and was in turn rammed by a
trireme from Aegina. But the Samothrakian marines, who were armed with javelins,
emptied the Aiginetan deck and leapt aboard, thus enabling their oar crew to leave
their floundering ship and man the trireme (Hdt. 8.90.2).

Unfortunately, however, Herodotos is very vague on the actual naval tactics
employed by either side at Salamis. The only real impression of the engagement from
Herodotos' narrative is that it was a 'slogging match', with bow-to-bow ramming, not
boarding, the order of the day; there are no indications of brilliant tactical moves being
performed by either navy.

To carry out the *diékplous* successfully required plenty of sea room. Salamis Strait
is only about 1km wide (not reckoning with extensive shallows) at its two narrowest
points, and so unsuitably narrow for this tactic. Besides, if the 'heavier' triremes of the
Greeks meant they were stronger built, they could have better stood up to bow-to-bow
ramming. Moreover, Persian morale may have been low after a night spent pulling an
oar and because they had thought the Greeks were divided and on the verge of panic.

It seems probable that the Greeks initially outnumbered the leading or western
wing Persian triremes, which included those of the Phoenician contingent opposite
the Athenians (Hdt. 8.85.1), and were able to cut them off and drive them ashore
before turning on the left or eastern wing and driving it out to the open sea – the
east–west alignment of the two fleets is confirmed by Aischylos (*Pérs.* 399), as against
the north–south alignment of Diodorus Siculus (11.18.1), which some scholars have
adopted (more recently by Morrison, Coates and Rankov 2000: 57–59, Hale 2009:
88, 91). Although originally numbering 300 triremes (Hdt. 7.89.1), the Phoenician

Salamis Strait, looking towards
the islet of Áyios Yeóryios from
the Paloúkia–Pérama ferry. This
narrow ribbon of blue water
allowed the Greeks, despite their
inferior numbers and heavier
triremes, to slog it out with the
invading Persian armada and
severely maul it. Beyond the islet,
on the Attic mainland stands
Mount Aigaleos where Xerxes sat
upon his silver-footed *díphros*
(more a stool than a throne) for
his ringside view of the battle.
(© Nic Fields)

contingent may now have been much reduced by storm and battle. All that we know for sure is that the Persian fleet suffered a bloody repulse: Aischylos (*Pérs.* 424–28) compares the final stage of the battle to a tunny catch, a particularly brutal and bloody affair.

As for the losses on both sides, notoriously Herodotos is entirely silent on the issue (just as Aischylos), but figures are preserved, or at any rate produced, by Diodorus Siculus: 40 Greek ships lost and more than 200 on the Persian side, 'not including those which were captured together with their crews' (11.19.3). The loss of more than 200 triremes with some 35,000 oarsmen would be a calamity for which Aischylos' summing up 'there never perished in a single day so great a multitude of men' (*Pérs.* 431–32) appears hardly dramatic enough. If on top of everything the ships in question happened to be mainly Phoenician with the most skilled crews in either fleet, the Persian losses that day were beyond doubt damaging. Within two months of his embarrassment at Salamis, Xerxes was in Sardis, the satrapal capital on the eastern edge of the Greek world. At the same time, the majority of the marines wintering in Kyme and Samos 'were Persians or Medes' (Hdt. 8.130.2), surely a necessary precaution if the Anatolian Greeks were feeling the urge to raise a new rebellion so as to bring about their liberty and freedom from the Achaemenid yoke.

Tomb of Dareios I at Naqš-e Rustam, near Persepolis, detail of the façade showing a Karian warrior. The Karian warriors aboard Artemisia's five triremes were armed very much like her Greek adversaries 'except they carried scimitars (*drépana*, literally 'sickles') and daggers' (Hdt. 7.93). This Karian, however, carries what appears to be a *xiphos*. (A. Davey/Wikimedia Commons/CC BY-SA 2.0)

# THE EURYMEDON (467/466 BC)

The battle of the Eurymedon (the precise dating of which is notoriously difficult to pin down) took place near the river of the same name, in Pamphylia, southern

The Eurymedon (modern Köprüçay), near Aspendos. The Eurymedon Bridge was a late Roman structure, the foundations and spoila of which were used by the Seljuqs to build this replacement bridge in the 13th century, the Köprüpazar Köprüsü. It was in the vicinity of the mouth of the river that Kimon defeated the Persians in a double battle, first at sea and then on land. (Adam Franco/Wikimedia Commons/CC BY-SA 2.0)

# ARTEMISIA (*fl.* 500–480 BC)

The vivacious Karian queen and indomitable Persian admiral Artemisia was a favourite subject of Herodotos. Among surviving ancient literature, Herodotos was the first to mention her, providing the most detail.

Artemisia was likely born around 520 BC in Herodotos' native Halikarnassos (now Bodrum), what was then the capital of the Karian satrapy of the Achaemenid Persian empire. She was a member of the Lygdamid dynasty (520–450 BC) of Halikarnassos, as the daughter of Lygdamis, a Karian, and his wife, a woman (unnamed by Herodotos) from Crete (Hdt. 7.99.2). She married the king of Halikarnassos sometime around 500 BC, just prior to the Ionian Revolt. Her husband, whose name has been lost to history, probably died only a few years later. They had a son named Pisindelis, who was still a boy when his father died. Taking the throne for herself, she made her name not as an ally of the Greeks, but as a dedicated subject of the Great King of Persia. Her realm included Halikarnassos and its hinterland, and the nearby islands of Kos, Kalymnos, and Nisyros.

When Xerxes went to war against Greece, Artemisia was the only woman among his commanders. As Herodotos is keen to point out, having a grown-up son meant there was no reason for her to take part in the expedition, and her 'own spirit of adventure and manly courage (*andrēíēs*) were her only incentives' (7.99.1). The Karian contingent of 70 triremes included Artemisia's. She brought five triremes, and those five ships carried with them a reputation for ferocity and valour (Hdt. 7.99.2). Herodotos hints that the Great King picked the Karian queen to lead a squadron so as to embarrass the Greeks, and indeed, when they heard about it, the Hellenic League offered an extraordinary bounty of 10,000 drachmae (about 30 years' wages for an ordinary workman) for the capture (presumably alive) of the Karian virago because they could not (or did not want to) believe a woman would join a war against them. No one succeeded in claiming the prize (Hdt. 8.93.2).

According to Herodotos (8.68–69) she was a woman of valour who unsuccessfully urged Xerxes not to fight at Salamis. Even so, the warrior queen of Halikarnassos fought bravely that fateful day, as she had done previously 'in the sea battles off Euboia' (Hdt. 8.68α.1), and her major claim to fame occurred during this naval engagement, which Xerxes observed from his silver-footed stool on the shore. Finding herself trapped between the deadly Greek triremes and the utterly bewildered Persian fleet, she determined to break out and reach the open sea. Closely pursued by an Athenian trireme she calmly and expertly rammed an allied trireme blocking her exit, and swiftly made her escape.

This ill-fated vessel turned out to be from Kalynda, which carried the Kalyndian king, Damasithymos – if true, the trireme was not only an ally but one of those actually under Artemisia's command (Hdt. 7.99.2). Herodotos says (8.87.3) he did not know whether she knew this and had some quarrel with the man, or whether it was an accident. Anyway, Ameinias, the Athenian *triērarchos*, confused by her actions, assumed she was either a Greek ship or a deserter from the Persians, and left Artemisia's ship to chase other prey (Hdt. 8.87.2–4). Had the Athenian realized who he was chasing, and recalled the price on her

Calcite jar, an *alabastron* (London, British Museum, inv. 132114), bearing the signature of Xerxes, discovered in 1857 in the ruins of the Mausoleum of Halikarnassos. (JMiall/Wikimedia Commons/CC BY-SA 3.0)

head, he would not have changed course. Believing Artemisia had despatched an enemy vessel, Xerxes was impressed at her nerve and daring, exclaiming: 'My men have turned into women, my women into men' (Hdt. 8.88.3). Apparently the ship was lost with all hands.

Beyond Herodotos, there are other references to Artemisia in Thessalos of Kos (*Presbeutikos* 27.5–6),

Polyainos (8.53.4), Aristophanes (*Lys.* 671–75, *Thesm.* 1200), and Justinus (2.12.23–24). Her grandson Lygdamis II was in power *c.*465–450 BC (Fornara 70). This was the Lygdamis, son of Pisindelis, who executed the epic poet Panyassis, the uncle of Herodotos, in 461 BC, after an unsuccessful uprising against him, which forced Herodotos to flee Halikarnassos.

Detail showing the signature 'Xerxes: The Great King', in Egyptian hieroglyphs, and three lines of lightly scratched cuneiform (Old Persian, Elamite and Babylonian). Of Egyptian origin, the presence of this jar in this location strongly suggests it was given by the Great King to Artemisia I, who passed it down to her descendants who eventually deposited it at the Mausoleum. Built for Mausolus (r. 377–353 BC) by his sister-wife Artemisia II around 350 BC, the Mausoleum was reckoned to be one of the Seven Wonders of the World in antiquity. (Marco Prins/ Wikimedia Commons/CC0 1.0)

Anatolia.[4] It was a double battle, fought near the mouth of the river and on land: both battles were won by Kimon, the Athenian *stratēgós*, who destroyed several Phoenician triremes. The Athenian dead were buried with all due ceremony in the Kerameikos, Athens (Paus. 1.29.14).

The three main accounts, provided by Thucydides, Diodorus Siculus, and Plutarch, differ in many important details. Thucydides (1.100.1) offers a quite brief account in which he reports a double victory on the same day and the capture and destruction of 200 Phoenician triremes. Cornelius Nepos (*Cim.* 2.2–3) mentions a double victory, by sea and by land, on the same day, but erroneously sets it near Mykale on the Anatolian mainland opposite Samos, rather than on the Eurymedon river. Diodorus Siculus first reports an Athenian naval victory off Cyprus

---

4    Diodorus Siculus places the battle in 470/469 BC, which is clearly mistaken; scholars usually suggest a date around 467 BC or 466 BC.

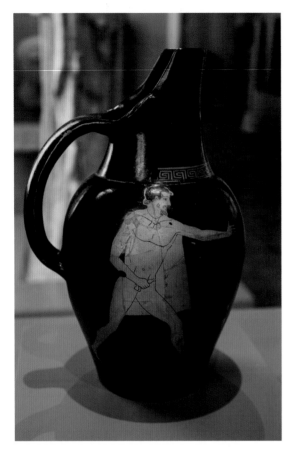

The Attic red-figure *oinochoe* known as the Eurymedon Vase (Hamburg, Museum für Kunst und Gewerbe, inv. 1981.173), attributed to the circle of the Triptolemos Painter and dated to *c*.460 BC. Amy Smith offers a comprehensive analysis of the pictorial content as an illustrative metonym for Greek triumph over a foreign army, specifically in terms of Kimon's victory over the Persians at the Eurymedon River, which had finally seen off the Persian threat to mainland Greece and the Aegean (Smith 1999: 135–36). (ArchaiOptix/Wikimedia Commons/CC BY-SA 4.0)

(11.60. 6–7), and then a long and complicated trick by which Kimon won a battle by land during the night (11.61). Finally, in an extensive account quoting historians such as Ephoros, Kallisthenes of Olynthos, and Phanodemos – Thucydides, though not named, is also used – Plutarch (*Kim.* 12.2–13.3) provides a number of details unknown to the other sources.

Though Thucydides' account is generally to be favoured, there may be some truth in Plutarch's assertion (*Kim.* 12.4–5) that the Persians were waiting for the reinforcement of 80 Phoenician triremes sailing from Cyprus, the base for a Persian reserve fleet. This might possibly explain why Kimon was able to launch a pre-emptive strike at the Eurymedon, where he first defeated the Persian fleet and then landed his marines to rout a numerically superior Persian army. Not content with this double achievement, he at once turned on the Phoenician reinforcements, practically annihilating them, though Thucydides does not mention this subsidiary action. Nonetheless, Kimon became famous as the one *stratēgós* who won a victory on sea and on land on the same day (Paus. 1.29.14).

# KIMON (c.510–451 BC)

Kimon was the son of Miltiades, the celebrated Athenian statesman and *stratēgós*, and Hegesipyle, the daughter of the Thracian chieftain Oloros and a relative of the Athenian historian Thucydides (Hdt. 6.39.2, Plut. *Kim.* 4.1).

In his youth he had the reputation of being dissolute, a hard drinker, and blunt and unrefined; it was remarked that in this latter characteristic he was more like a Spartan than an Athenian, even naming one of his twin sons Lakedaimonios (Thuc. 1.45.2, Plut. *Kim.* 16.1). Nonetheless, during the battle of Salamis Kimon distinguished himself by his bravery. Plutarch records that prior to the battle he had led a procession of his fellow *hippeîs* up to the Acropolis 'to dedicate to the goddess there the horse's bridle which he carried in his hands, signifying thus that the *polis* needed then not knightly courage but sea fighters' (*Kim.* 5.2).

Coming to the fore in the decade following the failure of Xerxes' invasion, Kimon used his wealth and influence to rebuild and refine Athens, which had recently suffered at the hands of the invading Persians. His energies were directed to public buildings, defences, and new facilities for his fellow citizens (Plut. *Kim.* 13.7–8). According to Pausanias (1.28.3), Kimon was instrumental in fortifying the Acropolis with walls. As Themistokles' stock sank ever lower, Kimon's rose ever higher.

Abroad Kimon was a successful *stratēgós*, and several of his campaigns against the Persians – in Thrace, on Skyros, and at the Eurymedon River (Thuc. 1.98.1–2, 1.100.1, Plut. *Kim.* 7.1, 12.6–13.5) – resulted in further adornments of Athens.

Like so many local heroes before him, Kimon eventually fell foul of the terrifyingly fickle Athenian *dēmos*. Sparta had appealed for aid in its war against the Messenians (Fourth Messenian War), and Kimon had a difficult time persuading the Athenians to help (Plut. *Kim.* 16.8). In 461 BC Kimon returned home only to find himself ostracized, which was to open the way for the next prominent Athenian statesman, Perikles. Yet Athens was to recall Kimon before the ten years of mandatory exile expired (Plut. *Kim.* 17.6), for the help he provided against Sparta during the First Peloponnesian War (460–445 BC).

Kimon's last overseas expedition was to Cyprus in 451 BC, with the purpose of retrieving the late debacle in Egypt. Here, while before the walls of Kition (a Phoenician

Modern portrait bust of Kimon on the seafront of Larnaka, Cyprus. Kimon died before the walls of Kition (at the centre of present day Larnaka), a Phoenician and Persian stronghold on the southern coast of Cyprus. He was buried in Athens, where a monument was erected in his memory. . (Markus Leupold-Löwenthal/Wikimedia Commons/CC BY-SA 3.0)

and Persian stronghold on the southern coast of Cyprus), ill health or the effects of a battlefield wound carried him off (Thuc. 1.112.2–4).

After Kimon's death there was no more open warfare against Persia. Instead there was a phase of 'Cold War', that grey space between normal state relations and hot conflict, with Persia practising the indirect *modus operandi* of economic and political subversion. In doing so, the Great Kings were employing their enormous wealth to finance and manipulate the squabbles of one Greek state against another. As Herodotos saw it, the Greek states were like lean mice while the Persian fat cat looked on.

# STATISTICS AND ANALYSIS

There is a passage in Xenophon's treatise on household management in which he uses the example of a trireme to illustrate the point that in the home the speedy movement and good order are important:

> And why else is a trireme laden with human beings a fearful thing for enemies and for friends a thing worth looking at, unless it is because it sails quickly? And how else do those who sail in it keep out of one another's way unless it's by sitting in order, bending forward in order, drawing back in order, and embarking and disembarking in order? (Xen. *Oikon*. 8.8 Bartlett)

In Xenophon's judgement, the trireme's principal virtue was speed under oar. Still, Xenophon must not in any way be taken for a naval expert. True, he had served in the Athenian *hippeîs* as a young man and later became a mercenary captain, but he never held an Athenian command, let alone a naval one. Themistokles, on the other hand, knew a thing or two about naval matters. After much argument (Hdt. 8.59–62), he persuades the Spartan admiral (*naúarchos*) to change his mind and adopt the plan of remaining, and ultimately fighting, where they were, that is, Salamis (Hdt. 8.63).

Themistokles' arguments, as set out by Herodotos (8.60α), are worth looking at in some detail. First, if Eurybiades chose to give battle at the Isthmus, this would mean fighting in the open sea. Second, fighting in the open sea was 'least advantageous' to the Greeks, with their 'heavier' (*barutéras*) and less numerous ships. As you would have thought, the difference in quality thus emphasized by Themistokles was taken for granted by the crews of the Persian triremes (Hdt. 8.10.1).

When Xerxes reached the Hellespont, the king was anxious to test the quality of his war fleet. He thus made a proclamation for a grand nautical gala, in which all who liked might contend. Each national contingent, no doubt priding themselves on their nautical skill being second to none, entered its best vessel for the coming race. The Great King himself, his grandees, generals and commanders, witnessed the victory of a Phoenician trireme hailing from Sidon, the largest and most important city on the Levantine coast during the Persian period. Xerxes, when he cared to venture upon the sea, was careful to embark aboard a Sidonian trireme (Hdt. 7.44, 7.100.2, cf. 8.118.1). In his catalogue of Xerxes' invasion armada Herodotos stipulates the Phoenician contingent was the largest and 'fastest' in the fleet, and of these triremes the Sidonian were the 'best movers (*árista pleoúsas*) in the water' (7.89.1, 7.96.1). Aischylos, in a round about way, confirms this when he says the Persian fleet contained 207 triremes 'excelling in speed' (*hypérkopoi táchei, Pérs.* 342–43).

It is not at all clear what 'heavier' ship means. It has been suggested (Morrison and Williams 1968: 134–35, Morrison 1991: 197, Morrison, Coats and Rankov 2000: 152) that whereas the Persian triremes had been hauled ashore and dried out on a wide beach near the mouth of the river Hebros near Doriskos (Hdt. 7.59.3), those of the Greeks had become fouled and waterlogged through being continuously in the water for perhaps as long as a year. Nevertheless, there is no reason why the Greeks should not have dried their ships out either before the Artemision campaign or in the interlude before Salamis, apart from the fact that Herodotos does not mention any attempt to do so. Paul Lipke, a professional maritime preservationist, views hauling a trireme out of the water to make it lighter by reducing the moisture content of the hull is a misconception. 'Any reduction in moisture content in planking below the waterline during hauling and "airing out", would be undone within a day or so of re-launching' (Rankov 2012: 205). The true benefit of hauling, he adds, was a means of combating shipworm infestation.

The action of 'drying out' almost certainly had much more to do with stopping leaks. Athens, remember, had built its new fleet of at least 100 and possibly 200 triremes in the short space of two years. Wherever the timber was obtained during these two years, very little of it can have been properly seasoned, though at least since the time of Homer (*Od.* 5.240) the Greeks were fully aware of the importance of not using unseasoned wood for shipbuilding. Albeit writing in the late 4th century AD, Vegetius advises against using unseasoned timber and warns that 'those (planks) fitted when still green exude their natural moisture and contract, forming wide cracks: nothing is more dangerous for sailors than for the planking to split' (4.36).

Another possibility is that the Greek triremes were 'heavier' in the sense that they were more solidly constructed. We have already made mention of Thucydides' comment (1.14.3) that the Athenian triremes that fought at Salamis, though the most recent built in Greece, were nevertheless old-fashioned in not having complete decks. It may well be that they were, in other respects, not built as well as the best in the Persian navy (viz. Phoenician). Ships built for speed and manoeuvrability, however, were actually at a disadvantage in confined waters, and it is possible that Themistokles had realized this fact as a result of the earlier Athenian experiences off Artemision. Indeed, at Artemision we are led to believe that the triremes of the Persian fleet were 'better sailing' (*ameinon pleoúsas*, Hdt. 8.10.1). Also, that the Persians were capable of carrying out the *diékplous* (Hdt. 8.9), a manoeuvre designed to row between the opposing ships and to turn hard about so as to ram an enemy vessel in the stern quarter. This does suggest that the Persian triremes were not only better built, but also their oar crews (viz. Phoenician) were better trained than were those of Greek triremes. Still, if the greenness of the timber or alternatively the solidity of construction made the Greek triremes heavier this was not a serious handicap in the narrow waters of Salamis.

Unfortunately Herodotos is very vague on the naval tactics employed by either side at Salamis (or Artemision). Herodotos does make the claim that the Hellenic League fleet at Artemision 'drew the sterns of their triremes together, their prows turned towards the barbarians' (8.11.1), and this would indicate a defensive measure. However, with 271 triremes this circular arrangement would have been rather large to say the least, and one wonders if triremes were capable of remaining in station in such a formation (cf. Thuc. 2.83–84). Again our knowledge of Salamis is limited with respects to battle tactics. The only real impression of the engagement from Herodotos is that it was a slogging match; there are no indications of brilliant tactical moves being made by either navy.

More to the point, if the 'heavier' triremes of the Greeks meant they were stronger built, they could have better stood up to bow-to-bow ramming. It is worth stopping here to remind ourselves that at the battle of Lade (494 BC) the Chian triremes were heavy with 40 hoplites serving as marines (Hdt. 6.15.1), which does suggest that the Greeks, at this particular naval engagement at least, relied on boarding more than ramming. On the other hand, in his detailed description of Sybota (433 BC), the naval battle that precipitated the Peloponnesian War, Thucydides says the style of fighting had been 'still in the inexperienced fashion' (1.49.1), that is, in contrast to the modern, rather one-dimensional mode as currently practised by the Athenians, which consisted in the use of the trireme herself as an offensive weapon. At Sybota, Thucydides continues, the triremes were crowded with hoplites, archers, and javelineers, and the engagement 'was more like a battle on land' (1.49.2) without any 'attempts to break the enemy's line (*diékplous*)', both sides (apart from the Athenian contingent of ten triremes) fighting 'with fury and brute strength rather than with skill' (1.49.3). In other words, the ships became locked together in a great crush and the hot work of the fight consisted of either marines repelling boarders or themselves boarding another vessel.

In the cold light of day Themistokles' arguments are by no means cast-iron. However, the withdrawal of the Hellenic League fleet to the Isthmus would have meant abandoning the last piece of Athenian territory, with no guarantee that the other Greeks would ever again assemble to fight for it. Lest we forget that the Corinthian admiral, Adeimantos, challenged Themistokles' right to speak at the war council since he had no 'fatherland' and was 'a man without a *polis*', a mere refugee. In reply to this insult, Themistokles casually pointed to the League fleet bobbing at anchor and said 'he had a greater *polis* than they' since he commanded 200 triremes fully manned with Athenian citizens (Hdt. 8.61.2, cf. 8.44.1). Athens contributed about half of the triremes in said fleet, giving it a great deal of influence.

# PERSIAN WARRIOR KINGS

The Persian Empire at the time of King Xerxes' rule (486–465 BC) was, without exaggeration, the greatest world empire to that date. At the corners of his empire ran the four great rivers of the known world: the Nile, the Ister (Danube), the Oxus (Amu Darya), and the Indus. Through the heart of his empire ran the Tigris and the Euphrates, rivers that had nurtured and nourished kingdoms and empires for centuries. The extent of this empire can be appreciated when Herodotos (5.50.2, 5.54.1) allows three months for a traveller from Sousa to Sardis, centre to western periphery. Indeed, so vast was Xerxes' domain that he could dream 'that the sun will not look down upon any land beyond the boundaries of what is ours' (Hdt. 7.8γ.2).

But what did this mean in Persian military terms? Effectively, Persian armies had a strategic range of some 4,025km by 1,610km. The use of naval forces in support of ground operations also increased range and flexibility. This of course was very much a function of the ability of the Achaemenid administration to place the vast resources of the entire empire at the service of military operations, which from time to time was not always the case.

At the heart of the Achaemenid military organization was at all times 'the Great King, king of kings, king of lands (OP *dahyāva*) containing many men, king of this great earth far and wide … an Achaemenid' (XPa §2 = LACTOR 16.63), and Achaemenids made war. So, from the founder Kyros to the last Great King Dareios III, Achaemenid kings were expected to lead grand military enterprises in person. Accordingly, Xerxes personally led the invasion of Greece.

Impression from Achaemenid Persian cylinder seal (New York, Metropolitan Museum of Art) showing the Great King (Dareios or Xerxes) despatching a Greek hoplite. (Marco Prins/Wikimedia Commons/CC0 1.0)

# AFTERMATH

With the Persians finally checked in the Aegean, the *raison d'etre* of the Delian League had been accomplished. Yet the Athenian victory at the Eurymedon paved the way to a stricter form of hegemony over some, at least, of their former Greek allies in the Aegean Sea. Initially the leader, now the master of what was once an anti-Persian alliance, the Athenian argument for this overt imperialism was a simple one: all those who reaped the benefits of the Athenian empire (Gk. *archê*) – freedom of the seas and freedom from Persian aggression – should join and contribute to the Delian League. The Eurymedon victory also made a great impression, one notable example being the dedication of a bronze date palm (*phoinix*, a pun on 'Phoenicians') by Athens in Apollo's sanctuary at Delphi (Paus. 10.15.3). Invigorating this hegemonic system and military coercion was of course the Athenian trireme, a weapon providing mobility, speed and range.

Yet, spectacular as it was, Kimon's double victory was to be the acme of Athenian imperialism. In 459 BC Athens despatched 200 triremes to Cyprus. This armada was then ordered to proceed to the Nile Delta to support Inaros, the Libyan prince from the western desert who had brought about the revolt of Egypt, against Artaxerxes I (r. 465–425 BC), the Great King of Persia (Thuc. 1.104). The Athenians, along with their allies, brazenly sailed up the Nile and captured most of Memphis, confining the Persian garrison to the citadel known as the White Tower (Fornara 77, 78). After this initial success, Thucydides reports that 'the Athenians in Egypt and their allies stayed on and encountered all the vicissitudes of war' (1.109.1). He does not explicate beyond this intriguing yet pithy statement. Yet it does appear that Athens was expanding beyond the Aegean and into the eastern Mediterranean, forming an alliance, for instance, with the Phoenician maritime city of Dora (Tel Dor, Israel). Whether the alliance was a mutual agreement or one that Dora was strong-armed into,

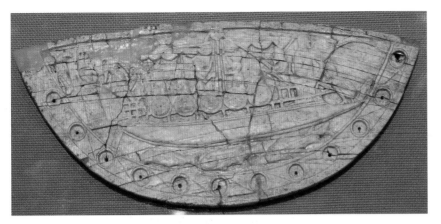

its sheltered harbour would have served as a well-located way station and naval base between Cyprus and Egypt. Dora, later described by Josephus as 'a fortress difficult to take' (*AJ* 13.7 §20), also had an unfailing freshwater spring.

Some five years later disaster struck the Athenians when the Persians annihilated their entire Egyptian expeditionary force in the Nile Delta. Shortly afterwards, a relief force of 50 Athenian triremes sailed into the Nile Delta in ignorance of what had befallen the original expedition, where most of them were cut off and captured. In another pithy statement from Thucydides: 'a few survivors of their great army found their way through Libya to Kyrene; by far the greater number perished' (1.110.1).

Following the Athenian shambles in Egypt, which was to be followed by setback in Cyprus (451 BC) and the death of Kimon, Diodorus Siculus (12.4.4–6, cf. Plut. *Kim.* 13.4–5) refers to the Peace of Kallias (449 BC). This was probably merely a tacit agreement between Athens and Persia to share spheres of influence. Thucydides does not mention this Peace of Kallias, and though our knowledge of it comes from references by the 4th-century BC Athenian orators Isokrates and Demosthenes, its existence was even challenged in antiquity.

As far as we can gather, Kallias, son of Hipponikos, the brother-in-law of Kimon, was given full authority to negotiate with Artaxerxes I. The Great King agreed to keep his naval forces east of the Chelidoniai, a small group of islands just south-east of the Hieron promontory on the south-west coast of Lykia, and east of the Kyaneai, two small islands at the place where the Bosporus meets the Euxine (Black Sea). The king thus tacitly recognized the Aegean Sea, the Hellespont, the Propontis (Sea of Marmara), and the Bosporus as Athenian waters, two of these waters, the Hellespont and the Bosporus, key chokepoints no less. In effect, the Graeco-Persian wars were over, but like the wild boar in Aesop's fable, which spent his leisure time whetting his tusks against a tree (he waits; he sharpens), the Athenian navy would not relax in time of peace. Every spring 60 triremes would put to sea and remained in active service for eight months of the year, which Plutarch (*Per.* 11.4) ascribes to Perikles' initiative.

For a brief period of 50 years Athens, a *polis* with an effective manpower of around 40,000, forcefully controlled the eastern Mediterranean and held in check the Persian Empire. As the Roman statesman and orator Cicero was later to explain in his *Fifth Philippic*, 'the sinews of war, money in abundance' (5.5). And this was the crux of Athens' maritime dominance, as Thucydides makes abundantly

Ostrakon (Athens, Ancient Agora Museum) bearing the name of Kimon, son of Miltiades. Kimon had proved himself to be an outstanding commander, both on land and sea, in the fight against the Persians, and his double victory on sea and land at the Eurymedon River seemingly put him at the summit of Athens' pantheon of heroes – but he would be ostracized in 461 BC for his pro-Spartan position. (Marsyas/Wikimedia Commons/ CC BY-SA 2.5)

clear. Wanting to avoid the need to fight on behalf of the Delian League many member states 'had assessments made by which, instead of producing ships, they were to pay a corresponding sum of money' (Thuc. 1.99.3, cf. Plut. *Kim.* 11.1–3, which tells the same story but the instigator is Kimon). This played into the hands of the Athenians. For the Athenian navy grew strong at their expense, and when states decided they no longer wanted to continue their membership, they found themselves at a clear disadvantage, lacking as they did the necessary resources or experience of war. All this was to end with the fall of Athens at the close of the Peloponnesian War in 404 BC.

# GLOSSARY AND ABBREVIATIONS

## Glossary

| | | | |
|---|---|---|---|
| | | | manoeuvre |
| *artemon* | 'boat' sail | *histion* | mainsail |
| *askōma/askōmata* | leather tubular sleeve(s) for oar-port | *histos* | mast |
| | | *hoplitēs/hoplitai* | 'fully-armed man' – hoplite(s) |
| *aulētēs* | double-pipe player | *hypēresia* | 'auxiliary group' – 14 armed men and 16 specialist seamen |
| cubit | unit of length (Attic = 0.444m, Doric = 0.49m) | *hypērésion* | cushion |
| *émbolos/émboloi* | ram(s) | *hypozōma/hypozōmata* | 'undergirdle(s)' – cable(s) to overcome hogging and sagging |
| *elatē* | silver fir | | |
| *epibatēs/epibátai* | 'deck soldier(s)' – marine(s) | *katástrōma* | deck |
| *epōtis/epōtides* | 'ear-timber(s)' | *kédros* | cedar |
| *diékplous* | 'through and out' – tactical | *keleustēs* | bo'sun |

| | |
|---|---|
| *kōpai* | oars |
| *kubernētēs* | helmsman |
| *kúklos* | 'circle' – defensive manoeuvre |
| *kypárissos* | cypress |
| mortise | recess cut to receive a tenon |
| *naupēgos* | shipwright |
| *naútēs/naútai* | oarsman/oarsmen |
| *nautikon* | navy, fleet |
| *oiax/oiākos* | tiller(s) |
| *pararrymáta* | side screens |
| *parexeiresía* | 'along-outside-rowing' – outrigger |
| *pēdalia* | steering oars |
| *pentēkontarchos* | 'commander of fifty' – purser |
| *perineō* | 'spares' – used of both oars and supernumerary personnel |
| *períplous* | 'around' – tactical manoeuvre |
| *peukē* | mountain pine |
| *pitys* | coastal pine (larch) |
| *plátanos* | plane |
| *plērōma* | ship's crew |
| *ploíōn* | ship |
| *prōratēs* | bow officer |
| *skalmós/skalmoi* | tholepin(s) – pin set vertically to serve as the fulcrum for an oar |
| tenon | hard wood rectangular block, each half-length fitting into a mortise |
| *thalamos* | ship's hold |
| *toxotēs/toxótai* | archer(s) |
| *triērarchos/triērarchoi* | trireme commander(s) |
| *triērēs/triērēis* | trireme(s) |
| *zyga* | thwarts – ship's main beams |

## Abbreviations

| | |
|---|---|
| *AcIr* | *Acta Iranica* |
| Aisch. | Aischylos |
| *Pérs.* | *Pérsai (Persians)* |
| *Supp.* | *Supplices (The Suppliants)* |
| *AJA* | *American Journal of Archaeology* |
| Akk. | Akkadian |
| Ap. Rhod. | Apollonios Rhodios |
| *Argon.* | *Argonautika* |
| Ar. | Aristophanes |
| *Ach.* | *Acharnenses (Acharnians)* |

| | |
|---|---|
| *Av.* | *Aves (Birds)* |
| *Ekkl.* | *Ekklesiazusai (Assembly women)* |
| *Eq.* | *Equites (Knights)* |
| *Lys.* | *Lysistrata* |
| *Ran.* | *Ranae (Frogs)* |
| *Thesm.* | *Thesmophoriazusai (Women Celebrating the Thesmophoria)* |
| *Vesp.* | *Vespae (Wasps)* |
| Arist. | Aristotle |
| *[Ath. pol.]* | *Ἀθηναίων πολιτεία (Constitution of the Athenians)* |
| *Part an.* | *De partibus animalium* |
| *Pol.* | *Πολιτά (Politics)* |
| Ath. | Athenaios |
| Bible | Books of the Bible |
| Ezek. | Ezekiel |
| Gen. | Genesis |
| Judg. | Judges |
| 1 Kgs. | 1 Kings |
| Clem. Al. | Clemens Alexandrinus |
| *Strom.* | *Stromateis* |
| *CQ* | *Classical Quarterly* |
| Diod. Sic. | Diodorus Siculus |
| Eup. | Eupolis |
| Eur. | Euripides |
| *Hel.* | *Helena (Helen)* |
| *HF* | *Hercules furens (The Madness of Herakles)* |
| *IT* | *Iphigenia Taurica (Iphigenia Among the Taurians)* |
| *Tro.* | *Troades (Trojan Women)* |
| *FGrHist* | F. Jacoby, *Die Fragmente der griechischen Historiker* (Berlin & Leiden, 1923–1958) |
| Fornara | C.W. Fornara (ed.), *Translated Documents of Greece and Rome I: Archaic Times to the End of the Peloponnesian War* (Cambridge, 1983) |
| Gk. | Greek |
| *G & R* | *Greece & Rome* |
| Hes. | Hesiod |
| *Op.* | *Opera et Dies (Works and Days)* |
| Hdt. | Herodotos |
| *Hist.* | *Historia, Zeitschrift für alte Geschichte* |

| Hom. | Homer | *Ages.* | *Agesilaos* |
|---|---|---|---|
| *Il.* | *Iliad* | *Artax.* | *Artaxerxes* |
| *Od.* | *Odyssey* | *Kim.* | *Kimon* |
| *IG* | *Inscriptiones Graecae* (Berlin, 1923–) | *Per.* | *Perikles* |
| | | *Them.* | *Themistokles* |
| Isok. | Isokrates | Soph. | Sophokles |
| *JHS* | *Journal of Hellenic Studies* | *Aj.* | *Ajax* |
| Joseph. | Josephus | Strab. | Strabo |
| *AJ* | *Antiquitates Iudaicae* | Theophr. | Theophrastos |
| LACTOR | London Association of Classical Teachers – Original Records | *Char.* | *Characteres* (*Characters*) |
| | | *Hist. pl.* | *Historia plantarum* (*Enquiry into Plants*) |
| Lat. | Latin | | |
| *MM* | *The Mariner's Mirror* | Thuc. | Thucydides |
| Nep. | Cornelius Nepos | Virg. | Virgil |
| *Cim.* | *Cimon* | *Aen.* | *Aeneid* |
| NIV | New International Version, 1984 | Xen. | Xenophon |
| | | *Anab.* | *Anabasis* (*The March Up Country*) |
| OP | Old Persian | | |
| Ov. | Ovid | [*Ath. pol.*] | *Respublica Atheniensium* (*Constitution of the Athenians*) |
| *Met.* | *Metamorphoses* | | |
| *Tr.* | *Tristia* (*Lamentations*) | *Kyr.* | *Kyroupaideia* (*The Education of Kyros*) |
| Paus. | Pausanias | | |
| Polyb. | Polybios | *Hell.* | *Hellenika* (*A History of My Times*) |
| Pl. | Plato | | |
| *Alk.* | *Alkibiades* | *Oikon.* | *Oikonomikos* (*Economics*) |
| *Grg.* | *Gorgias* | XPa | Xerxes inscriptions from Persepolis (a) |
| *Leg.* | *Leges* (*Laws*) | | |
| Plin. | Pliny (the elder) | XPf: §4 | R.G. Kent, *Old Persian. Grammar, Texts, Lexicon* (New Haven, 1953) |
| *HN* | *Naturalis historia* | | |
| Plut. | Plutarch | | |

# BIBLIOGRAPHY

Balcer, J.M., 1995. *The Persian Conquest of the Greeks, 545–450 BC*. Konstanz: Universitätsverlag Konstanz

Basch, L., 1969. 'Phoenician oared ships'. *MM* 55/2: 139–62

Casson, L. and Steffy, J.R. (eds.), 1991. *The Athlit Ram*. College Station, TX: Texas A&M University Press (The Nautical Archaeological Series, 3)

Cawkwell, G.L., 2005. *The Greek Wars: The Failure of Persia*. Oxford: Oxford University Press

Fields, N., 2007A. *Ancient Greek Warship 500–322 BC*. Oxford: Osprey Publishing (New Vanguard 132)

Fields, N., 2007B. *Thermopylae 480 BC: Last Stand of the 300*. Oxford: Osprey Publishing (Campaign 188)

Fields, N., 2008. *Syracuse 415–413 BC: Destruction of the Athenian Imperial Fleet*. Oxford: Osprey Publishing (Campaign 195)

Gabrielsen, V., 1994. *Financing the Athenian Fleet: Public Taxation and Social Relations*. Baltimore, MD: John Hopkins University Press

Green, P., 1996. *The Greco-Persian Wars*. London: University of California Press

Hale, J.R., 1973. 'Cushion and oar'. *The Oarsman* 5/2 and 5/3

Hale, J.R., 1996. 'The Lost Technology of Ancient Greek Rowing'. *Scientific America* 274/5: 82–85

Hale, J.R., 2009. *Lords of the Seas: The Epic Story of the Athenian Navy and the Birth of Democracy*. London: Viking Penguin

Hammond, N.G.L., 1956. 'The Battle of Salamis'. *JHS* 76: 32–54

Hammond, N.G.L., 1960. 'On Salamis'. *AJA* 64: 367–68

Hammond, N.G.L., 1982. 'The Narrative of Herodotos VII and the Decree of Themistocles at Troizen'. *JHS* 102: 75–93

Hammond, N.G.L., 1986. 'The Manning of the Fleet in the Decree of Themistokles'. *Phoenix* 40: 143–48

Hammond, N.G.L. and Roseman, L.J., 1996. 'The Construction of Xerxes' Bridge Over the Hellespont'. *JHS* 116: 88–107

Head, D., 1992. *The Achaemenid Persian Army*. Stockport: Montvert

Lazenby, J.F., 1993. *The Defence of Greece, 490–479 BC*. Warminster: Aris & Phillips

Meiggs, R., 1982. *Trees and Timber in the Ancient Mediterranean World*. Oxford: Oxford University Press

Morrison, J.S. and Williams, R.T., 1968. *Greek Oared Ships, 900–322 BC*. Cambridge: Cambridge University Press

Morrison, J.S., Coates, J.F. and Rankov, N.B., 2000 (2nd edn.). *The Athenian Trireme: The History and Reconstruction of an Ancient Greek Warship*. Cambridge: Cambridge University

Pritchett, W.K., 1959. 'Towards a Restudy of the Battle of Salamis'. *AJA* 63: 251–62

Quinn, J.C., 2018. *In Search of the Phoenicians*. Princeton, NJ: Princeton University Press

Rankov, N.B. (ed.), 2012. *Trireme* Olympias: *The Final Report*. Oxford: Oxbow Books

Sekunda, N.V., 1992. *The Persian Army 560–330 BC*. Oxford: Osprey Publishing (Elite 42)

Shaw, J.T. (ed.), 1993. *The Trireme Project. Operational Experience 1987–90. Lessons Learnt*. Oxford: Oxbow (Oxbow Monograph 31)

de Souza, P., 2003. *The Greek and Persian Wars, 499–386 BC*. Oxford: Osprey Publishing (Essential Histories 36)

Strauss, B., 2004. *Salamis: The Greatest Naval Battle of the Ancient World, 480 BC*. London: Hutchinson

Wallinga, H.T., 1993. *Ships and Sea-power Before the Great Persian War: The Ancestry of the Ancient Trireme*. Leiden: E.J. Brill

Wallinga, H.T., 2005. *Xerxes' Greek Adventure: The Naval Perspective*. Leiden: E.J. Brill (Mnemosyne, Bibliotheca Classica Batava. Supplementum, vol. 264)

Welsh, F., 1988. *Building the Trireme*. London: Constable

# INDEX